The New
Enchantment of America
GEORGIA

By Allan Carpenter

CHILDRENS PRESS, CHICAGO

ACKNOWLEDGMENTS

For assistance in the preparation of the revised edition, the author thanks:
ALPHONSO L. ROSSER, Information Specialist and JEANNE MCKOWN, Information Officer, Georgia Bureau of Industry and Trade.

American Airlines—Anne Vitaliano, Director of Public Relations; *Capitol Historical Society*, Washington, D.C.; *Newberry Library*, Chicago, Dr. Lawrence Towner, Director; *Northwestern University Library*, Evanston, Illinois; *United Airlines*—John P. Grember, Manager of Special Promotions; Joseph P. Hopkins, Manager, News Bureau; Carl Provorse, *Carpenter Publishing House*.

UNITED STATES GOVERNMENT AGENCIES: *Department of Agriculture*—Robert Hailstock, Jr., Photography Division, Office of Communication; Donald C. Schuhart, Information Division, Soil Conservation Service. *Army*—Doran Topolosky, Public Affairs Office, Chief of Engineers, Corps of Engineers. *Department of Interior*—Louis Churchville, Director of Communications; EROS Space Program—Phillis Wiepking, Community Affairs; Charles Withington, Geologist; Mrs. Ruth Herbert, Information Specialist; Bureau of Reclamation; National Park Service—Fred Bell and the individual sites; Fish and Wildlife Service—Bob Hines, Public Affairs Office. *Library of Congress*—Dr. Alan Fern, Director of the Department of Research; Sara Wallace, Director of Publications; Dr. Walter W. Ristow, Chief, Geography and Map Division; Herbert Sandborn, Exhibits Officer. *National Archives*—Dr. James B. Rhoads, Archivist of the United States; Albert Meisel, Assistant Archivist for Educational Programs; David Eggenberger, Publications Director; Bill Leary, Still Picture Reference; James Moore, Audio-Visual Archives. *United States Postal Service*—Herb Harris, Stamps Division.

For assistance in the preparation of the first edition, the author thanks:
Consultants Ruby H. Crowe, Social Studies Consultant, Fulton County Schools and C.T. Trowell, South Georgia College; Carroll Hart, Director, State Department of Archives and History; Claude Ivey, Office of State Superintendent of Schools; Stanley Bergquist, Office of State Superintendent of Schools; and Miriam K. Clum, Director of Curriculum, Clarke County Board of Education.

Illustrations on the preceding pages:
Cover photograph: Okefenokee Swamp, Georgia Bureau of Industry and Trade, Tourist Division
Page 1: Commemorative stamps of historic interest
Pages 2-3: The Okefenokee Swamp, Georgia Bureau of Industry and Trade, Tourist Division
Page 3: (Map) USDI Geological Survey
Pages 4-5: Atlanta area, EROS Space Photo, USDI Geological Survey, EROS Data Center

Project Editor, Revised Edition:
  Joan Downing
Assistant Editor, Revised Edition:
  Mary Reidy

Library of Congress Cataloging in Publication Data

Carpenter, John Allan, 1917-
  Georgia.

  (His The new enchantment of America)
  SUMMARY: Presents the history, resources, famous citizens, and points of interest in the Empire State of the South.
  1. Georgia—Juvenile literature.
[1. Georgia] I. Title. II. Series.
F286.3.C3 1979   975.8   79-12095
ISBN 0-516-04110-X

Contents

Stone Mountain State Park

A True Story to Set the Scene

PROCESSION OF IMMORTALS

"You are cordially invited to a breakfast on the shoulder of Robert E. Lee, signed Gutzon Borglum." There never was an invitation just like that, but the event actually did take place and is only a part of one of the most intriguing of the many stories of the enchantment of Georgia.

It all began when Mrs. Helen Paine, president of the Atlanta Chapter of the United Daughters of the Confederacy, had an idea to place on Stone Mountain a memorial to General Robert E. Lee and to the Confederacy. Stone Mountain, near Atlanta, in its own right is one of the geological wonders of the world—the largest single granite boulder in existence. Will Rogers once called it a pebble that California threw at Florida and missed.

Mrs. Paine and her group called in sculptor Gutzon de la Mothe Borglum, showed him the mountain, and suggested he carve on it a 10-foot (3-meter) relief figure of General Lee. Said the sculptor: "That would be like pasting a postage stamp on the side of a barn." The ladies were offended, but sculptor Borglum soon came up with the most breathtaking plans for a sculpture since the ancient Egyptians carved their vast temple of Abu Simbel.

Borglum himself described the plan, "It seems to me that the only fitting memorial to the South of 1861-65 by the equally great South of today, is to reconstruct as best we can the great characters of those days, and in colossal proportions, carve them in high and full relief, in action, mounted and on foot, ... following the mountain contour, moving naturally across its face to the East. These figures should be in scale with the mountain; they must be visible and easily read for miles; and their likeness must be recognized. ..."

Mary Borglum, the sculptor's wife, amplified her husband's description of his plan: "... sweeping downward and across were the Confederate armies mobilizing around their leaders. Above were artillery appearing at the summit as if coming from beyond, and dropping down over to the left across the precipice is the lifelike procession of men, guns, and horses. On the left of these were the cavalry in full motion, while in the center, where the cliff bulged outward, was the colossal group, two hundred feet (60.9 meters) in height, representing the principal chieftains of the Confederacy, among them Robert E. Lee, Stonewall Jackson, and ... Jefferson Davis. Swinging away to the left were the columns of the Confederate infantry."

The plan for this colossal procession was accepted, with the expectation that it would take ten years and cost three million dollars. The Stone Mountain Monumental Association was organized, and Samuel H. Venable, his sister, and nieces donated the entire northeast side of the mountain, valued at a million dollars. In 1916 the site was dedicated as a memorial, but World War I halted the work.

In 1923 Borglum began by inventing a giant triple-lens projector. It threw the outline of his figures on the mountain, and the projected outlines were drawn in white paint. By 1924 the head and shoulders of General Lee were finished. Fifteen thousand people gathered, and when the figure was unveiled the likeness was so striking that many people wept.

Borglum invited twenty outstanding leaders to join him for a breakfast celebration. Hal Steed, author of *Georgia: Unfinished State,* described the scene: "He seated his distinguished guests at tables set on Lee's massive shoulder. This was a publicity gesture—and a knockout. Not every layman could take in the artistic scope of the project. But to the dullest imagination the spectacle of a human figure so huge that a group could dine comfortably on its shoulder was sensational. The sheer audacity of the conception left them breathless."

Borglum and his workers, mostly tombstone carvers, swarmed over the rock for sixteen months. By February, 1925, more than half of the central area was roughed out; the head of Lee was finished and Stonewall Jackson's face was ready for final carving.

Then funds became low; a group of Atlanta businessmen gained control of the project, and Borglum heard that they were planning to dismiss him and get along with only the stonecutters, now that his masterwork had created all the plans and worked out all the details of

The carving on Stone Mountain, completed in 1970.

construction. In a rage the artist smashed the model of the work, destroyed his plans and fled across the state line just ahead of the sheriff. As one writer says, "the South lost a work of undoubted genius." Gutzon Borglum, of course, went on to immortality by creating the great sculptured figures on Mount Rushmore in South Dakota.

Sculptor Augustus Lukeman was employed to finish the Stone Mountain work. He made a much reduced new design of Jefferson

11

Davis, Lee, Jackson and a color bearer marching across the mountain. He said that Borglum's work was out of proportion and had it blasted away. In 1928 the Lukeman head of Lee was unveiled. There was bitter criticism. "Borglum's head of Lee everyone recognized," mourned the mountain's donor, Samuel H. Venable. "Lukeman's head of Lee few people recognize. The nose is crooked, the left arm looks withered and paralyzed, the hilt of the sword is gone; the stirrup of his saddle is broken off. The money is all gone and the Lukeman carving is mutilated."

The work was halted, and the unfinished carving remained like a scar on the vast mountainside for thirty-five years. Then in 1958 the state of Georgia bought the entire Stone Mountain region for $2,000,000. A $1,600,000 motel was built, and a $737,000 building was constructed on top of the mountain. Swiss engineers built a lift with a car capable of carrying fifty passengers to the peak. The park includes a plantation-house complex of prewar buildings, a replica of the *General,* famed wartime locomotive, five lakes, beaches, a game ranch, golf course, amphitheater, antique auto museum, sculpture garden, and a carillon from the Coca-Cola New York World's Fair pavilion. The cost of this huge recreation area exceeded $11,000,-000.

But the "star attraction" had not been forgotten. Sculptor Walter Kirtland Hancock was engaged to incorporate the unfinished Lukeman design into a new plan. He and his workers used space-age jet torches, generating white-hot heat, to melt the stone away and complete the sculpture. The fierce heat of the kerosene-oxygen flame could cut a 3-inch (76-millimeter) wide strip 4 feet (1.2 meters) deep and 20 feet (6 meters) long into the granite in only two and a half hours. This is 100 percent quicker than older methods, and the torches left a smooth, uncracked surface. Smaller torches were used for the details.

When completed in 1970, the 138-foot (42-meter) high picture in stone, even though much reduced from Borglum's original masterpiece, had become the largest portrait sculpture ever made. Lee's sword, 58 feet (17.7 meters) long, would weigh 100 tons (90.% metric tons) if separate.

12

Lay of the Land

Colorful Georgia sweeps from the warm sands of its Golden Isles to the cool mists of its Blue Ridge Mountains, with much that is also colorful in between. Georgia is the largest state in land area east of the Mississippi River. Experts divide it into five separate parts: Coastal Plain, Piedmont Plateau, Blue Ridge Province, Valley and Ridge Province, and the Appalachian Plateau. Generally, however, it is said to have three main regions—Coastal Plain, Central Plateau, and Northern Mountains.

The Coastal Plain region covers almost 60 percent of the state. Its surface was filled and formed when, over a period of centuries, tremendous quantities of soil, rocks, gravel, sand, and stone were washed down from the highlands. At the edge of this region is a real "wall." This is one of the country's most interesting features of geography—the Fall Line. A rise of land or ridge separates the coastal regions from the plateau across the country from south to north. Here the waters of rivers cascade or "fall" down from the higher region.

The middle region above the Fall Line is usually known as the Piedmont Plateau. It takes in more than 30 percent of the state and has a broadly rolling terrain, cut by trenches of deep, narrow valleys and laced with streams and rivers. Occasionally large hills or mountains may be seen in this area, such as Kennesaw Mountain close to Marietta and Stone Mountain near Atlanta. These peaks were formed when the surrounding land eroded away and left the harder surfaces extending above the ground.

The smallest but most picturesque region of Georgia is the mountain area. The Blue Ridge Mountains rise in northeastern Georgia and the Cohutta Mountains in the west. Springer Mountain is the most southerly peak of the Blue Ridge. The Cohuttas are an extension of the Great Smoky Mountains to the north. Separating the Blue Ridge and the Cohuttas is the Appalachian Valley. Mount Enotah (sometimes called Brasstown Bald) is the highest peak in Georgia, rising to 4,784 feet (1,458 meters). Lookout Mountain is one of the best-known mountains, although it is really a type of plateau rising abruptly out of more level ground. Because of its great length and unique location, Lookout Mountain extends through three states—Tennessee, Georgia, and Alabama.

Mount Oglethorpe is the southernmost peak of the great Appalachian Mountain chain which extends from Georgia through Maine.

As the crow flies, Georgia's coastline is about 100 miles (about 161 kilometers). However, there are so many twists and turns and islands along the shore that the tidal shoreline along that coast stretches for 2,344 miles (3,772 kilometers). Georgia is especially proud of its "Golden Isles," basking in the warm sun. These islands include Tybee and Little Tybee, Skidaway, Ossabaw, St. Catherines, Sapelo, St. Simons and Little St. Simons, Jekyll, and Cumberland.

REINS FOR A RAINDROP

Three important rivers help to form the boundaries of Georgia— St. Marys to the south, the Savannah on the northeast, and the Chattahoochee along the west. The latter two are among the major rivers of Georgia; the others are Flint, Oconee, and Ocmulgee. The Ocmulgee and Oconee flow roughly parallel for many miles, then finally come together to form the Altamaha, Georgia's largest river wholly within the state. The Oostanaula and Etowah rivers meet near Rome to make the Coosa River, not far from where it leaves the state for Alabama.

The Ogeechee, Canoochee, Satilla, Alapaha, and Ochlocknee are other Georgia rivers. One of the most famous of southern rivers— the Suwannee—has its beginning in the Okefenokee Swamp.

Although the Suwannee starts close to the Atlantic, it flows through southern Georgia to the Florida border and finally empties into the Gulf of Mexico. This is because the high rise of ground which divides Georgia's waters, so that some go to the Atlantic and some go to the Gulf, swings almost to the coast. The St. Marys, which rises almost as far west as the Suwannee, flows to the Atlantic.

Georgia's main watershed is formed by the Chattahoochee Ridge.

14

Riding on the sands of Georgia's "Golden Isles."

It is said that half of the roof of a house on this rocky backbone may send its water to the Gulf of Mexico while water from the other half may flow directy into the Atlantic.

Even more strange is the fact that a divide in the northwest sends the state's waters into the Mississippi River system. The Toccoa River is part of the Tennessee River system, so through it some of Georgia's waters flow into the Tennessee, then into the Ohio, down the Mississippi and into the Gulf, after a roundabout course.

Few states have had their rivers so well developed. Most of the major rivers have been controlled by one or more dams. This provides deeper channels for shipping, keeps the water levels more even throughout the year, creates waterpower and wonderful new recreation areas, and, probably most important, controls the floods

15

that once did so much damage throughout the state. As someone once said, "We have put reins on our raindrops."

All of the fine lakes in Georgia are man-made. These include Hartwell and Clark Hill reservoirs on the Savannah, both shared with South Carolina; lakes Seminole, Walter F. George, and Goat Rock, on the Chattahoochee, all shared with Alabama; Allatoona, Jackson, Nottely, Blue Ridge, and Chatuge reservoirs, and Lakes Burton, Rabun, Sinclair, Harding, Blackshear, Worth, Trahlyta, and Seminole. Lake Sidney Lanier, formed by Buford Dam, has been called "one of the most-visited sporting lakes in the United States." Thousands of small ponds are scattered over the Georgia landscape. They are used for irrigation, fishing, and watering places for cattle. Coffee County alone has 3,000 ponds.

There are also many springs in Georgia such as Magnolia, which flows with many gallons of crystal water a day, and famous Warm Springs, with its curative waters.

"Part lake, part land and part a mixture of both, but all moody, grand and mysterious," is one description of Okefenokee Swamp, which covers 660 square miles (1,709 square kilometers) of southeastern Georgia and is the largest undrained freshwater swamp in the United States.

THE ANCIENT LAND

At some far-off time the Okefenokee region was probably merely a saltwater sound, an arm of the Atlantic. As the centuries went by, the entrance to the sound was shut off by a reef; the salt water drained away, and today's swamp slowly emerged.

Many changes have come to the land now known as Georgia. On several occasions in the distant past, it was almost completely under the waters of ancient seas. Southern Georgia was probably under water when the present Appalachian Mountains were pushed upward inch by inch over the eons. These mountains are among the oldest on the globe; they once must have been at least double their present height, but water, wind, and frost have worn them down.

16

Long before the Appalachians were formed, another uplift created an ancient mountain chain over what is now Georgia's Piedmont Plateau. These mountains were almost completely worn away to gently rolling country.

One of Georgia's principal landmarks, Stone Mountain, was formed about 200,000,000 years ago, according to geologists. Somewhere below the earth, a mass of white-hot material formed and pushed its way toward the surface. Then this material cooled and hardened to become a vast hump of granite. When softer materials around it washed away in rain and flood, Stone Mountain emerged as a great rounded boulder on the skyline.

Gradually animal life came to the land, and as these creatures died, the bones of some became preserved to endure over the centuries. The first fossil discovered in Georgia was that of a giant ground sloth, found in 1823 on Skidaway Island by Samuel L. Mitchell. Later, mammoth, mastodon, hog, hippopotamus, ox, and horse fossils were found. Fossils of oysters almost 2 feet (.6 meters) in length and even a toothed whale have been uncovered. The fossil teeth of sharks are fairly common in the southern part of the state. One of the shark teeth was 6 inches (152 millimeters) long. Petrified wood has been found in southern Georgia.

CLIMATE

The Atlantic's Gulf Stream on the east and the Appalachian Mountains to the north help give Georgia the world's best climate zones. Georgia has seven of the nine zones of climate found in the United States. Because of the relatively low humidity, sunstroke and heat prostration are almost unknown in the state.

Rainfall throughout the state averages nearly 50 inches (127 centimeters) per year.

The Great Temple Mound at Ocmulgee National Monument, Macon.

Footsteps on the Land

VOICE OF THE EAGLE

Sprawled for more than 120 feet (36.6 meters) across the ground near Eatonton lies the body of an eagle, wings outspread. The outline of this majestic bird has been formed by carefully placed rows of stone and earth. Every feature—tail, head, neck, beak—is in perfect proportion. The best way to see the shape of this great eagle is from a helicopter.

However, this figure was made centuries before the day of helicopters. Who its builders were no one will ever know. Another mystery is how such primitive people were able to form what one expert called the "most perfect effigy mound in America." Effigy mounds are those built in the form of animals or people. They are just one type of the thousands of mounds that are found throughout Georgia. Most of what we know about people who lived before written records were kept is discovered by studying such mounds and the materials excavated from them.

The second largest prehistoric mound in the United States is the main so-called Etowah Mound near Cartersville. It covers 3 acres (1.2 hectares) and rises as high as 65 feet (19.8 meters). Experts think that a temple rested on the top of this mound. Sculptured metal plates, pottery with colored designs, and jewelry of a type made in Mexico and Central America are among the unusual items found at Etowah.

When the Lamar Mounds were cut into, the layers showed that at least six different groups of people formed them over the years between 8000 B.C. and A.D. 1717. These peoples have been named Wandering Hunters, Shellfish Eaters, Early Farmers, Master Farmers, Reconquerors, and the Indians known to history. Kolomoki Mounds, near Blakely, have given up many articles made by the Early Farmers. At Nacoochee Mounds pottery and other items have been found indicating that their makers were quite advanced.

Prehistoric peoples of Georgia left other evidence of their presence beside the mounds. At Ocmulgee National Monument near

Macon there is a prehistoric cornfield. After centuries the hummocks where the corn was planted can still be seen, along with two paths. Such a prehistoric garden is so unusual that there are only two in all of North America.

Post holes and parts of the foundations have been found which tell much about the houses and buildings of these early peoples. At Lamar it can be seen that the houses were about 25 feet (7.6 meters) wide; posts held up a roof which was apparently thatched and covered with a red clay. A pot of charred beans was found as well as some partly burned corncobs. Some authorities feel that walls and ditches on Brown's Mound made up an early fortress.

The most recent prehistoric peoples known to occupy the Lamar region are called the Hitchiti. They may even have been living in Georgia as recently as the early visits of Europeans.

An artifact found at the Etowah Indian Mounds at Cartersville.

LAND OF CREEK AND CHEROKEE

The Europeans, in the earliest written accounts, mention two main groups in what is now Georgia. These were the Cherokee and Creek. The original home of these people is unknown, nor is it known just when they arrived. Both Cherokee and Creek legends tell that their ancestors drove   N

Georgia. The Cherokee   d

throughout much of No   *Indians*   k

pushed on into the south   f

Alabama.

In regions where their   *tribe*

rivalry between Creek and

wars. In what is sometim

Cherokee gave a terrible

Cherokee preserves. At ot

settle disputes over territo

won the region south of th

games with the Cherokee

favorite games of the regi

ture of soccer, lacrosse, a

Early explorers found th   ... .gia region built permanent homes of cane or straight poles covered with clay as a sort of
plaster. These buildings were sometimes round, sometimes rec-
tangular. They had roofs of bark over bent cane framework. Indian
women planted and tended the simple crops which were mostly corn,
pumpkins, and beans. Fishing and hunting provided the rest of what
was generally a good living for Indian families of the region.

Indians of the area were not especially skilled in crafts until the
coming of the Europeans; then they became fine craftsmen in many
fields, including metalwork. This was especially true of the Cherokee. One of the interesting native crafts of the Cherokee was the
making of balls for their favorite game. The skin of a deer was
scraped, soaked, and packed with deer hair as nearly round as possible. This was sewed firmly with deer sinews and reminds present
observers somewhat of a baseball. The racket for this early form of

21

lacrosse was about 2 feet (.6 meter) long and was cupped like the palm of a hand.

There were many well-established Indian communities in Georgia. The Creek settlement of Standing Peachtree was on the south bank of the Chattahoochee about 7 miles (11 kilometers) from Atlanta. Another Indian town was Kashita, now the modern community of Cusseta. Thunderbolt was an Indian village near Savannah. It took its name from the legend that a spring flowed from the spot where the earth was struck by a lightning bolt.

Among the many interesting Indian myths are those of the legendary peoples they created in their active imaginations. One such group was the Yunwee Chuns Dee, which means little people. These inhabited the skies, and Indians claimed they sometimes heard their mysterious and magical music floating through the air. Another legendary group was the Nunne-hee. The Indians said they never could be conquered, and they were the "patron saints" of all who became lost or injured while traveling. They were supposed to be the special guardians of the Cherokee.

AN UNSETTLED LAND

Suddenly the Indians were confronted with a kind of people they could never have imagined. They marveled as an incredible procession made its slow and painful way. This was the expedition of Hernando de Soto, the Spanish conquistador who came with 500 Europeans and 200 Indian burden bearers on a search for gold.

The exact route of this great expedition probably never will be known. It is thought that in the year 1540 they entered Georgia in the southwest and angled across the state, leaving at about present-day Augusta. When they reached what is thought to have been the Ocmulgee River, one of the Indians was converted to Christianity and received the first baptism known to have taken place in Georgia.

De Soto turned northeast somewhere in South Carolina and angled back into Georgia at an unknown spot. He may have visited the Cherokee village of Guaxule on the Chattahoochee River. The expedition is thought to have spent a month on the site where Rome now stands and then marched out of Georgia by way of the Coosa River. This brief visit left a legacy of disease and suffering and cruel treatment of the Indians that was never forgotten by the peoples who suffered from it.

Other European explorers may have passed along the coast of Georgia before the time of de Soto, but he is the first one to make a record of exploring what is now the state. Spain claimed North America, but French explorers began to sail past and around Georgia's coastal islands. Most important of these was the red-bearded giant Jean Ribaut, who explored the region in 1562 and set up a colony called Port Royale. Some feel Port Royale was on the Savannah River. French explorers and trappers set up small temporary headquarters in various areas of Georgia.

In 1565, King Philip II of Spain sent Pedro Menéndez de Avilés to drive out the French and strengthen Spanish claims in the region. Menéndez viciously destroyed the French and built several forts on the islands. Then he moved to the mainland and pushed into the interior, followed by priests who tried to set up missions. He was fiercely met by the Indians, and within two years the Spanish were driven from the mainland. However, they kept their forts and missions on the islands.

The garrison on St. Catherines Island was established by Menéndez in 1566; San Jose Mission was built on Sapelo Island. In these and other locations the Spanish met the Indians on the mainland, and French and English attacks from the sea. In spite of this they remained, with the priests trying to teach and convert the Indians from their mission headquarters.

Tolomato Mission, on what is now known as Blackbeard's Island, across the creek from Sapelo, was one of the largest mission fortresses. Here the Indians began a widespread revolt against the Spaniards in 1595, but the Europeans managed to stay on.

In 1670 the French and English made an agreement against the Spanish that declared the region to be neutral ground. After this the area became a "haven for lawless adventurers." Pirates of both nations plagued and harassed the Spanish settlements. After more than a century of struggle to hold their settlements, in 1686 the Spanish finally retired below the St. Marys River. However, they refused to give up their claims to the region.

In 1716 a new flag flew over Georgia. The ugly pirate Blackbeard brought his crew to the island that now bears his name and hoisted the black flag over his new headquarters there. In addition to the pirates, there continued to be trappers and traders with the Indians in Georgia. Glass beads, brass bells, pistols, and old-fashioned guns found near Macon are thought to be from a trading post set up by traders from South Carolina sometime between 1690 and 1715.

King Charles II of England gave the coast of Georgia to the lords proprietors of Carolina, and in 1717 Scottish Sir Robert Montgomery started an unsuccessful colony between the Savannah and Altamaha rivers. The first English settlement in Georgia was built in 1721 near present-day Darien and named Fort King George in honor of the sovereign. His Majesty's Independent Company manned the fort to protect the English settlements to the north from the French and Spanish. At a much earlier date there had been a Spanish fort on the same site.

A BUFFER AND A HAVEN

In the early 1700s many Englishmen began to be concerned with injustice. They called the attention of Parliament to the condition of the honest poor people. When they could not pay their debts, people were thrown into jail; there, of course, they had no way of paying their debts and no way of getting out of jail. Parliament assigned one of its members, wealthy General James Edward Oglethorpe, to investigate this problem.

General Oglethorpe made a startling recommendation: to establish a crown colony in the New World as a home for deserving people, a "New Society," which has a surprisingly modern sound. He obtained the support of about nineteen other leaders, such as Viscount John Perceval, who was well known for his work among the poor. King George II signed a charter on June 9, 1732, providing a grant for "the land lying between the Savannah and Altamaha rivers and westward from the sources to the South Sea . . . for settling poor persons of London." The new colony was to be named Georgia in honor of the king.

Oglethorpe and his twenty associates became a board of trustees in complete charge of the affairs of the colony, including selection of the settlers and distribution of land to the colonists.

In addition to the welfare of the poor there were many other advantages for setting up such a colony. In England these people were a burden not only for themselves but for the mother country. In America they would be self-sufficient; they would have raw materials to sell and also would provide a strong new market for England's goods.

Even more important, prosperous South Carolina needed a buffer zone for protection against the Spanish, French, and Indians. Spain still claimed territory extending as far north of Florida as present-day Beaufort, South Carolina. The French had edged in from the Mississippi River and established themselves as far east as Fort Toulouse in Alabama. In 1715 the Indians had swept into South Carolina in what was known as the Yamassee War.

Because of all this, Georgia was established as the last of the thirteen original English colonies in America, and the only one of these to be founded mainly for humanitarian and military reasons. On February 12, 1733, the ship *Anne* sailed 18 miles (30 kilometers) up the Savannah River carrying General Oglethorpe and about 125 colonists; it dropped anchor opposite a high bluff. The weary passengers followed their leader to the top of this bluff. Waiting quietly to meet them was a group of Indians, headed by Chief Tomochichi. These were the Yamacraw, an outlawed branch of the Creek nation. In their honor the cliff still bears the name of Yamacraw Bluff.

About half a block from the site of the present-day city hall, a tired General Oglethorpe pitched his tent and rested for the night, and the others followed his lead. The next morning everyone began the business of creating a new colony. On May 21, Oglethorpe and Chief Tomochichi solemnly signed a treaty allowing the colonists to settle in the region. Mary Musgrove, who was half Indian, served as the

Oglethorpe's statue in Savannah.

interpreter. During all their long association, the Yamacraw never fought the British.

It is said that when he came ashore, General Oglethorpe had under his arm precise plans for laying out a new city. These had been prepared in England by Robert Castell. It is a strange irony of fate that Castell, the man who had planned a home for freed debtors, himself died in a debtors' prison.

The site the colonists had chosen for their settlement on Yamacraw Bluff looked out over a wide expanse of flat lands the Spanish called *sabana*, savannah in English, and so the new town was named Savannah. Assisted by Colonel William Bull, Oglethorpe built a primitive fort on the eastern end of the bluff. They laid out an orderly grid system of east-west, north-south streets. However, this grid was frequently broken by little green parks, called squares. In the early days, these squares were surrounded by rough pole fences so that the people could run to them for protection in case of attack.

A little more than a year after he had arrived, in April 1734, Oglethorpe returned to England to report to his colleagues, the trustees. With him went Chief Tomochichi, his wife, nephew, and other members of his groups. This foreign "king" was greeted with great excitement by the people of Britain. Tomochichi was received by the Archbishop of Canterbury in Lambeth Palace and by the king at Kensington Palace. The appearance of the Indians gained new support for the colony in England.

GROWTH AND CHALLENGE

In 1736 Oglethorpe and his guests returned to Georgia with a large group of colonists in what was known as the "Great Embarkation." The two ships that brought them were convoyed by the man-o'-war *Hawk* under Captain James Gascoingne. Two of the most interesting and unusual of the passengers were Charles and John Wesley. Altogether, between 1732 and 1740 more than 2,500 emigrants were sent to Georgia with funds provided by the trustees.

In addition to debtors, the trustees offered refuge to the persecuted Protestants of many European countries, and many of these arrived at this time and later.

At the end of this period, only eight years after the settlers first pitched their tents on Yamacraw Bluff, an English traveler was able to speak of the "fine houses" of Savannah. But there were many more accomplishments for this "infant among the colonies." Under Oglethorpe's direction, Fort Frederica was built; this has been called the "largest and most important in America." More than 2,000 volumes had been brought in to form a useful library. One of the most interesting accomplishments of the early colony was establishment of the first agricultural experiment station in the country, known as the Trustees' Garden.

In much of their work the colonists had the goodwill and assistance of Governor Robert Johnson of South Carolina, who was a friend of General Oglethorpe.

Among General Oglethorpe's greatest achievements was the making of eight treaties of peace with various Creek Indians. One of the most important of these came in 1739 with the Upper Creek at their village of Coweta Town, in present Russell County, Alabama. This confirmed the colony's title to the land between the Altamaha and Savannah rivers, increased the territory of the colony, and helped to keep the Creek from allying with the French or Spanish. The relations of the Georgia colony with the Indians were probably the most peaceful of all the colonies.

In 1739 England was once more at war with Spain, and the Georgia colonists soon began to feel the pressure of their Spanish neighbors to the south. For three years the two forces clashed; then on June 28, 1742, one of the largest war fleets to appear in American waters dropped anchor off the sandbar of St. Simons Island, with the Spanish flag fluttering in the breeze.

In the face of this show of force by the Spanish and their Indian allies, General Oglethorpe spiked the guns of St. Simons and retired to Fort Frederica, which was the strongest in the area, and the Spanish immediately captured St. Simons. In July, Oglethorpe, with a force of about nine hundred, including British marines, regular British troops, Scottish Highlanders, and Indians, drove the Spanish back as they approached Frederica. Then Oglethorpe pretended to retreat, but left an ambush party in the thick underbrush of the damp and marshy region. The Spanish, sure the English were giving up, stacked their arms and made ready to eat a meal.

Suddenly a Scottish tam was raised on a stick as a signal, and the British ambush party attacked. The Spanish lost two hundred men in what has come to be known as the Battle of Bloody Marsh.

This small battle has been called "one of the decisive battles of world history," because after this time the Spanish never again successfully pressed their claim to any coastal territory north of Florida, and from that time on Spanish expansion and fortunes in the New World continued to decline. The date of this battle was July 7, 1742.

One of the interesting sidelights of this war with Spain was the fact that a woman—Mary Jones—had the position of commander of Fort Wimberley, which guarded the narrow portion of the Skidaway River. She bravely defended the fort during the Spanish attack.

Fort Frederica, built under General Oglethorpe's instructions, is now a national monument.

General Oglethorpe went back to England in 1743, and he never again returned to his American colony.

Georgia had been the only colony where slavery and liquor were forbidden. The colonists resented this. They also felt that they did not have enough control of their own affairs in other ways. Many of the colonists were bitter about all of this, and there was considerable lawlessness. Many slaves were smuggled in. The liquor prohibition was repealed in 1742, and in 1749 slavery was legally introduced for the first time.

In 1752, when it appeared that the trustees were not going to be successful in their lofty aims and when they could not get the funds they needed, they turned the colony over to the king, and in 1754 Georgia became a crown colony. John Reynolds, first royal governor, served from 1754 to 1757. There were troubles with the Spanish and Indians. Ministers frequently had to station militiamen to guard the four corners of the church against Indians during the services. Also, there were many disputes over borders. South Carolina, for example, claimed much territory south of the Altamaha River.

At the Treaty of Paris in 1763, the western borders of Georgia were fixed. The southern boundary followed the St. Marys River to its source and from there westward to the meeting of the Flint and Chattahoochee rivers. There the boundary followed the Chattahoochee to the 31st parallel, from where it went westward clear to the Mississippi. The northern boundary remained uncertain at this time.

Life in Georgia changed very much during this period. Midway was settled by the Puritans. Many wealthy people from South Carolina and elsewhere bought the inexpensive lands of Georgia and moved there with their hosts of slaves. By 1766 there were about 10,000 white people and 7,800 slaves. The land that had originally been founded as a free home of free people now also had its laws providing penalties for debtors and its own debtors' prisons.

FROM TRAGEDY TO TRIUMPH; THE REVOLUTION

Many people of Georgia joined with the other colonies to protest what they felt were the unjust taxes laid on them by the mother country. As a royal colony, they suffered under strict rules and heavy payments. A local group called the "Liberty Boys" was formed to protest these and other "injustices."

There were many in Georgia who were loyal to the king (Tories), and when Georgia was asked to send delegates to the First Continental Congress, the Loyalists and the royal governor, James Wright, managed to keep the colony from sending delegates. This angered many of the other colonies. The Second Continental Congress met in May of 1775, also without Georgia delegates. Lyman Hall of St. John's Parish went to the congress on his own without any authorization and was accepted, but without power to vote. The other colonies agreed to have no further contact with Georgia under a ban called "colonial nonintercourse."

By June, however, a Council of Safety was appointed at Savannah; this elected delegates to the Continental Congress, and Georgia was welcomed into the united colonies. When the Declaration of Independence was approved, three Georgia delegates were among the signers: Button Gwinnett, George Walton, and Lyman Hall.

There were still many Tories loyal to England, but the royal governor had already fled to Halifax, Canada, on a Royal Navy ship, and there was great enthusiasm. The Liberty Boys raised the Liberty Flag on a liberty pole in front of Tondee's tavern at Savannah. The Liberty Boys swept aboard the British schooner *Phillipa* in Savannah Harbor and captured her. Soon another Liberty Flag flew from the *Phillipa's* masthead. A battalion of troops was organized at Savannah by Colonel Lachlan McIntosh, and militia were raised for local protection. In 1777 Savannah became the capital of the new state of Georgia.

In the next year, British Colonel Sir Archibald Campbell brought a force of about 2,000 troops to a landing a few miles below Savannah. American General Robert Howe had only 600 troops, but he thought the marshes in the region were almost impossible for the British to get through. However, Colonel Campbell found the secret passageways through the marsh with the help of local Tories who knew the region. In a surprise attack, on December 29, 1778, General Howe lost Savannah and a large number of his men to the British. General Howe was later court-martialed for this loss, but was acquitted of the charges.

The infant government of Georgia fled to Augusta as a temporary capital, and Governor Wright came back from exile to try to return Georgia to the status of a British colony. Soon after the fall of Savannah every principal town in the state fell into British hands. The capital was moved to Heard's Fort in Wilkes County.

During the British Revolutionary occupation it is said that Savannah and other parts of Georgia endured as much hardship as Atlanta and Columbus did later during the War Between the States. Food was scarce, and smallpox and other diseases took a heavy toll. One authority says the Americans "suffered untold hardships and cruelty at the hands of British and Tories." Prisoners were sometimes hanged or tortured to death. Most of the fighting in Georgia during this period of the Revolution was a form of guerrilla warfare.

Count d'Estaing, leader of the French fleet, tried to recapture

Battle of Fort Moultrie, *by John Blake White.*

Savannah, but he failed and lost nearly a thousand of his French and American troops. Among those killed in this battle were the popular patriot volunteer Count Casimir Pulaski and the Georgia hero of Fort Moultrie, Sergeant William Jasper.

The Americans retook Augusta for a short time, but Tory Colonels Grierson and Browne soon brought it back into British hands. Browne and others had been tarred and feathered by the patriots early in the war, and the Tories were able to take revenge on many who had humiliated them. Augusta was almost entirely ruined during the war and had to be rebuilt. Fort Augusta was even renamed Fort Cornwallis by the British.

Then the tide slowly began to turn for the Americans. One of the most unusual stories of warfare was the engagement at King's Ferry in October, 1779. Colonel John White, Captains A. G. Elholm and George Melvin, and a force of only three other soldiers planned to capture a British force of one hundred thirty men and five ships under the British commander Captain French. They planned to fool the British into thinking they had a very large force. All through the night they built fires and called out loudly to nonexistent sentinels. Colonel White then rode boldly alone up to the British and demanded their immediate and unconditional surrender.

The relieved British officer thanked him for sparing his men and they surrendered. The six Americans burned the five ships, rounded up the prisoners, and took them off to prison camp.

A more important victory came at Augusta. American Cavalry

General Henry (Light-Horse Harry) Lee, father of Robert E. Lee, was faced with the task of capturing Fort Cornwallis (Augusta) where the British had held out for many months. General Lee remembered that ancient warriors built a kind of wooden tower from which they were able to "rain destruction on their enemies." He had such a tower built, and his men were able to rake the inside of the fort with their fire. The fort fell and once more Augusta was in American hands.

General Nathanael Greene had been placed in charge of American forces in the South. He sent General "Mad" Anthony Wayne to recapture Savannah. In 1782 the daring General Wayne, along with the Georgia Legion and the forces of Colonel Twiggs, was able to force the British out and take possession of Savannah on July 11, 1782. British rule had ended forever in Georgia.

STATEHOOD

Many writers have pointed out that the poverty of the people of Georgia brought on by the war was "appalling." However, they soon began to recover. The northern boundary of Georgia was fixed along the 35th parallel in 1783, and Georgia extended its laws into present-day Mississippi. The Georgia district of Natchez was set up. Two years later Bourbon County was organized along the Mississippi.

In 1787, after generations of dispute, the troublesome boundary line between Georgia and South Carolina was finally fixed. In the same year, Georgia sent six delegates to a convention which was to consider changing the Articles of Confederation. These articles were the government of the United States at that time. After an entirely new constitution was written, two of these delegates, William Few and Abraham Baldwin, signed on behalf of Georgia the new Constitution of the United States.

On January 2, 1788, a Georgia convention unanimously ratified the United States Constitution, becoming one of only three states to approve the new Constitution without one vote against it. With this act, Georgia, the thirteenth colony, became the fourth state.

Yesterday and Today

A new state constitution was approved in 1789. Augusta at this time was the temporary capital of Georgia, but the new town of Louisville was being laid out for the capital, which was moved there in 1795. Other events of the period included the popular visit of President George Washington in 1791 to Augusta and Savannah and the invention of the cotton gin near Savannah by Eli Whitney. The census of 1790 showed Georgia's population to be 82,548.

One of the strange events in Georgia history was the Yazoo Act of 1795 in which Georgia "sold" 35,000,000 acres (14,164,000 hectares) of its claims in Mississippi and Alabama at a price below a cent and a half per acre. There was such a scandal about this land giveaway that the act was canceled. In an odd ceremony in front of the capitol building at Louisville in 1796, all the documents concerning the Yazoo Act were publicly burned as a symbol of the error that had been made. However, in 1802 the Georgia claims in Alabama and Mississippi were finally given up to the United States by the Treaty of Fort Wilkinson.

Most of the action of the War of 1812 in Georgia was concerned with the southern Indians who had been stirred up by the British. However, a number of Georgia Indians gained high position in the United States Army. The Uchee chief, Timpoochee Barnard, reached the rank of major. Chief William McIntosh led his Lower Creek Indians against the British.

There was so much growth and development in Georgia after the war that the period has been called the "Golden Age of Prosperity." The Atlanta region was first settled in 1813, and the community grew with amazing speed. The steamship *Enterprise* sailed from Savannah to Augusta in 1816. Only three years later Georgia played a great part in the history of transportation. On May 22, 1819, the ship *City of Savannah* left its namesake city and after an epic voyage reached Liverpool in England. This was the first ocean crossing ever made by a ship equipped with steam power.

Opposite: The Allatoona Dam and powerhouse on the Etowah River.

A TRAIL OF TEARS

A series of wars with the Indians was waged between 1817 and 1821 mostly in Florida with the Seminoles, but fighting sometimes extended into the region around the lower Flint and Chattahoochee rivers. General (later President) Andrew Jackson finally succeeded in ending this warfare.

When Georgia gave up its western lands in 1802, the United States had agreed that the state should receive title to all Indian lands within the state. However, the Creek and Cherokee had highly developed civilizations. They had prosperous farms, fine houses, towns, and even slaves; they had no intention of giving up the land they had lived on for generations.

In 1824, Georgia Governor George M. Troup told the United States that it must live up to its treaty and force the Indians out. President Monroe called the Creek chiefs, led by Chief William McIntosh, to a conference at Indian Springs in 1825. The Creek agreed to give up all their Georgia lands for four hundred thousand dollars and a similar amount of land west of the Mississippi. Other Creek leaders, not at the conference, denounced Chief McIntosh and said that he had no right to deed away their lands. The Indians held a great council and sentenced Chief McIntosh to death. A group of one-hundred-seventy Indians searched and found him and carried out the execution. Much of the difficulty with the Indians came about in such a way. An agreement would be made with one group and another group would declare that the first had no authority to make an agreement.

President Monroe was inclined to take the side of the Indians, but Governor Troup threatened that if the Indians were not removed Georgia would go to war with the United States. Soon new treaties were signed, and the Creek left Georgia for their new home.

The Cherokee had established an entirely separate nation. The Appalachian Valley was the center of this nation, with its capital at New Echota. The Cherokee government operated under a constitution similar to that of the United States. Its diplomats were received at Washington in the same way as diplomats from other "foreign" countries. When Indian foe Andrew Jackson became president, this situation quickly changed. In 1828 Georgia declared it was in control of the Cherokee territory; gold hunters and settlers rushed in. The Indians were forbidden to hold meetings, and those who objected were removed or killed. By 1832 the state had divided most of the Indian land into homesteads and raffled off the Indian property to homesteaders.

The federal government offered the remaining Indians new homes in the West plus a payment of five million dollars for their entire nation. Because they could do nothing else, the Indians accepted. Major Ridge, a Cherokee chief who signed the agreement, was later executed as Chief McIntosh had been. Most of the money was never paid to them. Chief Joseph Vann was forced from his beautiful home; more than thirteen thousand other Cherokee were ruthlessly rounded up like cattle in 1838 and marched off on a tremendously hard journey overland. So many died on this trip that the route is still known as the "Trail of Tears." A few Cherokee escaped into the higher mountains and their descendants remain today on the Cherokee reservation in North Carolina.

John Howard Payne, composer of "Home Sweet Home," tried to help the Indians and was thrown in jail, charged with sedition. Moravian missionaries had been teaching the Cherokee since 1800. When they attempted to go to the aid of their Indian friends, they were tried and sentenced to the state penitentiary, where they were held for more than a year until the United States Supreme Court freed them.

TRIUMPH AND TRIBULATION

Slavery had been dying out in Georgia until Eli Whitney invented the cotton gin there. When it was possible to grow vast quantities of cotton for a profit, it was desirable to obtain the largest possible numbers of workers at the cheapest cost. This meant a large increase in the number of slaves used to work the rapidly increasing number of cotton plantations.

An 1829 law made it a crime to teach either free or slave blacks to read and write. However, many blacks were skilled in carpentry, masonry, wagon making, and other trades. In 1845 all black mechanics were forbidden by law to enter into any contracts for such services.

In the North there was growing complaint about the treatment of blacks in the South. There are those who say that if both sides had been more temperate the situation might have been changed, with justice for all, without the horrible suffering that followed. This was not to be, however.

As the first of the other Southern states declared their secession and left the Union, cannon were fired in celebration in various Georgia towns. In January, 1861, a convention met at the Old State House in Milledgeville, then the state capital, to consider Georgia's secession. Former Governor Herschel V. Johnson, Ben Hill, and Alexander Stephens were against secession, but T.R.R. Cobb thundered to the members, "We can make better terms out of the Union than in it." When the vote came on January 19, it was 208 to 89 in favor of Georgia's withdrawal from the United States. Georgia became the fifth state to secede and join the Confederate states. T.R.R. Cobb was a principal figure in drawing up the new Confederate constitution.

Georgia Governor Joseph E. Brown has been called "one of the boldest and most turbulent leaders in Georgia's political history." Before any other states had seceded he urged the Georgia legislature to do so, and even before the state voted to secede he ordered Fort Pulaski to be seized. Later he was able to get the Federal arsenal at Augusta to surrender, and in March men from Savannah seized Fort Jackson.

When President Abraham Lincoln called for 75,000 volunteer troops for the Union army, the *Macon Telegraph* printed huge headlines reading "War! War! War!! War!!! 75,000 Barbarians Coming Down on the South!" Georgia was the first state to send troops into Confederate service.

In April, 1862, Union forces landed near Fort Pulaski, guarding Savannah. They spent difficult days dragging large cannon across the marshes and placing them to face the fort. The Southern defenders were not worried. When the fort was built a young officer just out of West Point had helped in its construction. He had declared the fort was so well built its walls could withstand any attack. His name was Robert E. Lee. What he could not have known was that new kinds of rifled cannon would be developed. When the Union troops used such cannon in the attack on Fort Pulaski, they easily drilled through the fort's "impregnable" masonry walls. On April 11, Confederate forces in the fort under twenty-five-year-old Colonel Charles H. Olmstead surrendered. This was an important turning point in the long history of warfare. The traditional masonry fort was no longer effective. According to one expert, "the fall of Fort Pulaski marked a beginning of a new era in modern warfare."

With the fall of Fort Pulaski, Union forces were able to close the Savannah River and the port of Savannah to trade from the outside. Except for some action along the coast, little military activity occurred in Georgia in the early years of the war. One of the best-known episodes of the war began in Georgia on the same day as the fall of Fort Pulaski. A group of twenty-one Union soldiers under James J. Andrews disguised themselves as passengers and rode a train hauled by a powerful locomotive known as the *General.* When the crew and other passengers stopped for breakfast at Big Shanty (Kennesaw), the Union men seized the *General* and headed for Chattanooga.

The train crew started after them on foot, then found a handcar and finally took a switch engine. At Kingston they took another heavier engine, which they had to abandon because of a broken track. Keeping up the chase on foot the Confederate trainmen at last came to the *Texas,* one of the speediest engines of its time. It was facing the wrong way, but they continued the chase by chugging off in reverse in the direction of the fleeing *General.* The backward *Texas* speedily began to overtake the fugitives, who tried unsuccessfully to derail it by dropping ties and fuel on the tracks. At last the *General* and its Northern crew were captured. Andrews and some of his men were later executed in Atlanta as spies.

In May, 1863, Colonel Abel D. Streit made a dash from northeastern Alabama in an attempt to capture Rome. His force of 1,466 men was captured by only 410 men led by General Nathan Bedford Forrest, who tricked Streit into believing he was outnumbered.

After the fall of Chattanooga to Union troops, there occurred just across the border in Georgia a battle that has been called the "bloodiest two days of the war." This was the Battle of Chickamauga, beginning on September 19, 1863. Guides who take tourists around the battlefield today point out the locations where thousands died in the forested hills, and they speak even yet in hushed tones as they show places where the blood literally ran down the slopes. The Battle of Chickamauga is considered the greatest Confederate victory in the interior.

By the next spring, however, with Chattanooga as the base, the troops of General William Tecumseh Sherman began their attack on outnumbered Confederate forces led by General Joseph E. Johnston. Because of the greater Union strength, General Johnston could do little but withdraw, gaining as much time as he could. There were battles at Dalton, Resaca, and New Hope Church; then the Union Army was given a heavy loss in the Battle of Kennesaw Mountain.

General Sherman found he could not force his way into Atlanta, which had been fortifying itself since May. He began a campaign of what one writer has called "a sequence of maneuvers, engagements and sieges" through July and August, 1864. General Johnston was replaced by General John B. Hood. He threw caution to the winds in attacking the Union forces outside of Atlanta. Hood failed in his attacks at Peachtree Creek, July 20, in what was called the Battle of Atlanta on July 22, and at Ezra Creek on the 28th. The Union successes enabled Sherman to shut off systematically the sources of supply of the city, and in the Battle of Jonesboro on September 1 the last railroad was seized.

General Hood and his forces left Atlanta that night, and the mayor surrendered his city the next day. Later, Sherman ordered all residents to leave the city and after a night looting and roistering, Atlanta was burned. Of 4,500 buildings in the city at the beginning of the fire, only about 400 remained standing when the last ember flickered out.

The visitors' center at Kennesaw Mountain National Battlefield Park.

General Sherman next carried out his threat to march to the sea and sweep everything in the way before him. At the state capitol in Milledgeville, men of the Union forces held a mock session of the legislature in which they "repealed" the state's secession act. Scarcely anything of value was left in a 60-mile-wide (97-kilometer) swath across the state.

An unusual incident occurred in the Jones house at Birdsville near Millen. The soldiers had stripped the property and set it on fire. The lady of the house was ill and refused to move from her bed; if her house went, she said, she would go also. When the soldiers saw she meant what she said, they put out the fire and saved the house.

Augusta expected to be attacked and piled its cotton ready to be burned. However, for some reason, Sherman passed it by.

In December, 1864, General Sherman attacked Fort McAllister guarding the land approach to Savannah. This earthwork fort had withstood seven different attacks from the heaviest naval guns. Some of these attacks were the most spectacular of the war. The gallant garrison of only 230 men was at last overwhelmed by an entire Union division of about 4,000. After a march of 300 miles (483 kilometers) across Georgia, the Sherman land forces had made contact with Union naval forces on the coast; the Confederacy had been completely divided.

General Sherman's forces marched into Savannah on December 22, 1864. The general sent a telegram to President Lincoln offering him the city and its vast stores of supplies as a "Christmas present." The Union troops stabled their horses in Colonial Park Cemetery. They were ready to confiscate the chimes of St. John's Episcopal Church, but the people appealed directly to President Lincoln, and he ordered them saved. They may still be heard today.

Even after General Robert E. Lee surrendered in Virginia, Union troops under General James H. Wilson attacked and destroyed much of Columbus. However, there was such a tremendous store of cotton in the city (125,000 bales) that General Wilson found it impossible to burn. Columbus had been the second-most important city in the Confederacy in furnishing wartime necessities. The gunboats *Jackson* and *Muscogee* had been made there; cannon, pistols, bayonets, sabers, powder, clothing, shoes, and food supplies had poured out of the city for the troops. However, the entire state of Georgia had been a vast arsenal of the Confederacy. As supplies grew lower, the people gladly contributed church bells and various household metals to be melted for casting cannons.

Fort Tyler at West Point was the last Confederate fort to fall during the Civil War. Wounded soldiers and older men, who did not know Lee had surrendered the week before, fought on gallantly. But the fort fell on Easter Sunday, April 16, 1865. Jefferson Davis held the last Confederate cabinet meeting in the Wilkes County Courthouse at Washington on May 5, 1865. After the meeting Davis left for a Southern port, but he was captured in a wooded section now named Jefferson Davis Memorial Park. After being brought to Macon, Davis was given a chance to escape, but he felt it would not be proper for him to do so, and he refused.

The fighting was over, and the last remaining Georgia troops were surrendered to General Wilson. More than 125,000 Georgia men had taken part in the struggle; numbers from Union County and elsewhere who were not in sympathy with the Confederacy had served on the Union side. The destruction, suffering, humiliation, and loss of life were beyond telling. The great wealth was gone; the plantation system and the other economic bases of the state had vanished; banks were wiped out; railroads and other transportation and communication were in shambles. General Sherman had estimated that the destruction of his march to the sea, alone, cost Georgia one hundred million dollars.

THE LONG ROAD BACK

The state bitterly submitted to President Andrew Johnson's terms to be readmitted to the Union, and a long "time of agony" followed. The terms included the emancipation of slaves, repudiation of the war debts of the Confederacy, and canceling of the secession ordinances of 1861. On October 26, 1865, Georgia repealed the secession ordinance by a convention held at Milledgeville. However, the state refused to accept the 14th Amendment to the United States Constitution, and military rule was established by Congress.

Under the supervision of the military government, a new constitution was written and accepted in an election, and the military leadership ended. Rufus Bullock became governor. The new legislature had thirty-two blacks among its members. Atlanta was chosen as the capital. The people of Georgia considered that these matters were being forced on them; they felt oppressed by the injustices of unscrupulous people known as carpetbaggers, who had come into the South to make their fortunes without much regard for the rights and welfare of others. Local people who took advantage of the situation were known as scalawags. The Union League and other organizations promoted activities that were hateful to many in the state. In their turn the Southerners formed the Ku Klux Klan, which soon terrorized blacks out of politics.

Governor Bullock felt that his authority was shaky, and when the legislature refused to accept the 15th Amendment, federal troops were again sent in for military rule. When the legislature accepted the 15th Amendment on July 15, 1870, Georgia was readmitted to the Union. After a long investigation by Congress, Governor

Bullock resigned in October, 1871, and hurriedly left the state, followed by most of the carpetbaggers and scalawags. Governor James M. Smith took office on January 12, 1872, and the period known as "Reconstruction" in Georgia was finally at an end.

A MODERN STATE

When the present state constitution was accepted in 1877, the people made Atlanta the permanent capital. In 1881 the International Cotton Exposition was held in that city, an indication of its new position of importance. The Party of the People or Populist Party became prominent and in 1888 elected Thomas E. Watson to Congress. He later became the party's candidate for president. In 1889 Gainesville became the first town south of Baltimore to have its streets lighted by electricity. The Ladies' Garden Club of Atlanta, founded in 1891, became one of the country's most outstanding organizations of its kind.

An unusual turn of events began in 1894 when Georgia sent relief supplies to the people of the Midwest who were suffering from a drought. Many Midwesterners were so touched by this kindness that they reversed the westward migration and moved to Georgia. Mr. P. H. Fitzgerald, editor of the Indianapolis, Indiana, *Tribune,* organized a stock company with a large group of old Union soldiers. They purchased 32,000 acres (12,950 hectares) of land in what is today Ben Hill County and planned, settled, and incorporated the city of Fitzgerald in 1896. Today the strong Midwestern character of the city is noticeable in its cultural life and in the pattern of roads, constructed in the precise north-south, east-west arrangement so characteristic of the Midwest.

Another cotton exposition, the Cotton States International Exposition, was held at Atlanta in 1895. One of the principal speakers at this exposition was black educator Booker T. Washington.

Three thousand Georgia men volunteered for service in the Spanish-American War in 1898. After the close of that war, President William McKinley visited a National Peace Jubilee in Atlanta. He spoke movingly of those who had died in the Confederate cause and did much to help restore good feelings.

The tragedy of a race riot struck Atlanta in 1907; that same year statewide prohibition was adopted, and this remained in force for thirty years. The Savannah River rose in a memorable flood at Augusta in 1908. On March 2, 1912, Georgia became the birthplace of one of the world's most important organizations for young people—The Girl Scouts of America.

During World War I, Atlanta was an outstanding center for troop training. In 1917, during the first year of that war, Atlanta suffered another disaster not connected with the war; a great fire destroyed more than 2,000 buildings in the city. Georgia's servicemen during the war numbered 93,321—plus 238 nurses; 525 died.

In 1924 a famous polio victim visited Warm Springs for the first time. He felt that the waters helped him. He was so taken with the area that he began a lifetime of personal association with it. This, of course, was Franklin Delano Roosevelt, who was later to become governor of New York and president of the United States. In 1927 Mr. Roosevelt established the Warm Springs Foundation.

During World War II, Georgia was one of the major centers of military activity. One of the country's great military reservations was Camp Gordon, near Augusta, named for General John Brown Gordon, Confederate leader. Great quantities of military supplies of all kinds passed through the port of Savannah on their way to various fronts. Savannah shipbuilding was stepped up so that during the war 88 Liberty Ships and more than 35 other vessels slid down the ways at Savannah to aid the Allied cause. Altogether more than 320,000 Georgians served in the armed forces during World War II, and 6,754 died.

An event that stunned the world occurred in Georgia on April 12, 1945. The famous portrait for which President Roosevelt had been sitting in the Summer White House at Warm Springs was never to be finished. He died just as the war that had sapped his strength for almost four years was coming to a successful close, after so many setbacks and such vast heartbreak.

The unfinished portrait of President Roosevelt at Warm Springs.

In 1952 Atlanta made a great gain as a leading metropolitan center with the annexation of 82 square miles (212 square kilometers) of territory, which added more than 100,000 to the city's population. The present state flag of Georgia was adopted in 1956; it is strikingly similar to the Confederate flag and in a sense might be considered a memorial to the Confederacy.

Another ship bearing the proud name of *Savannah* sailed into its namesake port in 1962. One Georgia writer reported, "The city's heart and the pride of the nation swelled with the maiden voyage visit of the world's first nuclear powered merchant ship. . . to her home port."

The Stone Mountain sculpture was finished in 1972, and Atlanta elected its first black mayor, Maynard H. Jackson, Jr., in 1973. However, for most Georgians the most outstanding event was the inauguration in 1977 of former Georgia Governor Jimmy Carter as president of the United States.

THE PEOPLE AND THEIR GOVERNMENT

The state constitution written in 1877 has served the state ever since, although in 1945 so many revisions were made in it that it was practically rewritten under the administration of Governor Ellis Arnall, who sponsored the changes. The governor was elected for a four-year term, and he could not succeed himself. However, this was changed in 1978.

The lieutenant governor presides over the state senate and is elected for a four-year term, as are the secretary of state, comptroller general, attorney general, state treasurer, superintendent of schools, commissioner of agriculture, commissioner of labor, and the five members of the Public Service Commission.

There are seven judges of the State Supreme Court and nine judges of the State Court of Appeals, all elected for six-year terms. The legislature is made up of two houses with both state representatives and senators elected for two-year terms.

Georgia has pioneered in a number of fields of government. In 1866 the state became the first in the Union to guarantee full property rights to married women. Of special interest to young people is the fact that Georgia was also the first to lower the official voting age to eighteen.

As early as 1736, in addition to English people, the Georgia colony included Swiss, Italian, Portuguese, French, Irish, German, and Scottish people. The latter introduced the game of golf to Georgia. Members of the Jewish faith made the colony their home during the first year of its settlement. Those of other faiths included many who had been persecuted in Europe because of their Protestant beliefs. Notable among these were the Salzburgers from Bavaria. The

Georgia trustees paid their expenses when they came to the New World in search of religious freedom. Each Salzburger family was given 50 acres (20 hectares) and a mulberry tree, so that they could begin the cultivation of silk. The Salzburgers made highly desirable citizens because of the many skills they had in agriculture and as mechanics. They established the communities of Ebenezer and New Ebenezer. The *Georgia Guide* by George G. Leckie says that "Greed seems to have had no part in them; their attitude can be brought to a focus by saying that they turned their hands to work and their minds to God."

Another religious group to enter the state in 1752 was made up of large numbers of Puritans from Massachusetts.

As the years have gone by, almost every religion and nationality has been represented in Georgia, including an interesting group of French people from Santo Domingo who were loyal to the king and fled during the revolution there.

A common term of outsiders in referring to some Georgians and of some of the people in referring to themselves is "Georgia Cracker." There are many stories about the beginning of that nickname; however, the most reasonable seems to be that mule drivers hauling tobacco hogsheads from the growing areas in the north to Savannah snapped their long rawhide whips over the animals with a cracking sound. Because of this they came to be known as Georgia "Crackers." The path they took also became prominent as "Tobacco Road."

Some people feel that changes in the status of black people have come too slowly; others marvel that, in view of all the many difficult problems, changes have come about as quickly and peacefully as has been the case in Georgia.

Black and white alike have been swept up in an "industrial revolution" which has come about in a few years rather than in many generations as in other parts of the country. Populations have shifted, cities have mushroomed, and rural areas have decayed. In the midst of these changes all races and groups in Georgia have an opportunity to plan and work together for a future of increased status and rising hopes for everyone.

Natural Treasures

As a Seminole brave and his Cherokee sweetheart were eloping, so legend goes, she broke a twig from a bush. When she reached her new home she planted it; this twig sprouted and became a white rose with a yellow center—the Cherokee rose, the state flower.

Georgia boasts a profusion of other wild flowers including the tall pitcher plants, poinsettia, Confederate rose, hibiscus, camellia, and trailing arbutus. One of the most unusual plants is the strange evergreen named Franklinian in honor of Benjamin Franklin. The higher mountain areas have flowers normally found only much farther north. Blooms of rhodondendron and mountain laurel add their beauty to springtime in the highlands.

One of America's most important forest areas is that of the lower coastal regions. The finest stands of Georgia's longleaf pine at one time were reserved for the exclusive use of the Royal Navy to make the soaring masts of the fleet. Even today more than 60 percent of Georgia's total land is in forests, made up of 163 species of trees, including such hardwoods as oak.

Typical of the coastal South is the mighty live oak; Oglethorpe's oak at Darien is said to have sheltered an entire company of soldiers under its branches. Slash pine, cabbage, and saw palmetto are other typical trees.

Other trees include black oak, black walnut, Florida maple, hickory, northern red oak, red maple, scarlet oak, sourwood, southern red oak, swamp chestnut oak, swamp cottonwood, and white basswood.

The location of the state and its varieties of climate make possible trees of both north and south. Among the more "exotic" are the tupelo gum, bald cypress, and the rare Ogeechee lime tree of the swampy underbrush. The brilliant stems of redbud blossoms punctuate the somber hillsides. Flowering quince, the striking red flowers of crepe myrtles, and the great waxy blooms of the stately magnolias provide another period of beauty. Spreading mimosa, sassafras, and chinaberry are other attractive trees.

In spring, Atlanta and other cities, as well as the country-

Providence Canyon in Lumpkin.

side, are transformed with the beauty of blossoming white dogwood trees, with here and there one of Georgia's native pink variety.

About the animals of Georgia, William Bartram, a naturalist, wrote in the 1770s, "The buffalo, once so very numerous, is not at this day to be seen in this part of the country; there are few elks, and those only in the Appalachian Mountains. The dreaded and formidable rattlesnake is yet too common. . . The alligator, a species of crocodile, abounds in the rivers and swamps near the seacoast, but it is not seen above Augusta. Bears, tigers, wolves, and wild cats are numerous enough." Today few of the large animals are found. Deer and bear almost vanished from north Georgia but they have been reintroduced through the efforts of such men as Arthur Woody, who devoted his life to restocking Georgia with deer. Beavers have returned in such numbers that in some areas they are considered pests. However, they are still one of the state's most important fur animals.

More than 350 species of birds are known in Georgia. In Okefenokee Swamp alone at least 90 species are known, including the popular anhinga or water turkey. Many birds such as the ivory-billed woodpecker, swallow-tailed kite, and Florida crane have almost disappeared. The wood duck at one time was almost gone, but fortunately has made a comeback, and the beautiful wild turkey is also increasing in numbers.

In south Georgia thousands of white cattle egrets migrate north from Florida in the spring and summer and share pastures and ponds with cattle. The first cattle egret was observed in the state in 1954.

Popular game birds are quail and dove, along with the marsh hen. The state has many wildlife refuges, including more than 1,500,000 acres (607,000 hectares).

In addition to the alligator, the most notable reptile is the sea turtle, which sometimes grows to 300 pounds (136 kilograms). Turtle egg hunts are a popular activity around Savannah in the season.

Other inhabitants of the sea include shrimp, crab, and oyster, as well as a wonderful variety of fish for deep-sea sportsmen. There are at least twenty species of game fish caught along the Georgia coast, including magnificent tarpon, striped bass, shad, jack crevalle, cobia, bluefish, and Spanish mackerel. Popular freshwater fish are rainbow, brook, and brown trout, walleye, pickerel, crappie, large and smallmouth bass, catfish, and bluegill. One of the more unusual fish is the goggle-eyed perch.

The Georgia Game and Fish Department is developing state-sponsored fishing ponds such as McDuffie Public Fishing area, where families can enjoy good fishing.

The most important minerals of Georgia are granite, marble, and clay. Several areas are especially well known for their minerals. One of these is the Bartow County mineral belt, centered at Cartersville, with a wealth of manganese, talc, limestone, iron, potash, cement, slate, and bauxite. The first discovery of bauxite in the country was made in Floyd County in 1887.

Right: Cotton is still one of Georgia's most important crops. Below: Sweet sorghum, grown in Georgia, is made into syrup by pressing the juice from the stems and boiling the juice.

People Use Their Treasures

AGRICULTURE

If you were to ask a Georgia farmer if he had "gone chicken," the reply likely would be, "Yes." Georgia leads the nation in the production of poultry of all types. It ranks second behind Arkansas in the production of chickens of the "broiler" type. That industry is centered about Gainesville, which calls itself the "World's Poultry Capital." Another region of broiler production is developing in south Georgia, with Douglas as the hub.

Georgia also leads the nation in production of peanuts and pecans. The state is also first in lima beans for fresh market, velvet beans, and blue lupine seeds. Ninety-five percent of America's pimiento peppers are grown and packed in Georgia. Peanuts began to gain in importance when the boll weevil cut down cotton production. In addition to food and oil, peanuts are now being used in a large variety of chemical processes. The Georgia Peanut Company at Moultrie processes a third of all the nation's edible peanut products. The first pecan orchard in the state appears to have been that of Jim Bacon at De Witt. Today the industry is so advanced that technical devices such as mechanical shakers are used. These are attached to the trees to shake down the nuts.

While cotton is no longer king, it still is one of Georgia's most important crops. Presently cotton ranks below peanuts in overall income to the state, but still exceeds the annual value of tobacco. The great decline in cotton brought about by the boll weevil was fairly well controlled by 1926. Among Georgia's most famous crops is sea island cotton, first introduced by Anne and Thomas Butler King on Sea Island. A stalk of cotton grown in Georgia in 1912 is said to be the world's largest. It had 715 bolls, as the individual puffs of cotton on the plant are called.

Georgia's start in agriculture was unique. The trustees of the colony planned an experimental garden to see which plants might be grown to provide the mother country with wines, herbs, silks, and other items she was forced to import. Gifts of seed of many kinds were sent to the trustees' garden, including the first cotton seed. Benjamin Franklin sent some rare seeds he had obtained from China. Coconut, bamboo, peach, orange, olive, fig, and pomegranate all were used in the experiments.

Because the silkworm will eat only mulberry leaves, every colonist in Georgia was required to plant mulberry trees. The first silk ever sent to England from the colonies came from Savannah and was used to make a dress for the queen of England. By 1764 silk culture in Georgia had reached it peak of 15,000 pounds (6,804 kilograms). Silk Hope near Savannah was a well-known silk plantation. Eventually, however, the silk industry declined.

Over the years, farming in general declined because the soil was exploited, and erosion ate away a vast number of acres. One spectacular example of erosion is known as the Little Grand Canyon of Stewart County. It covers about 3,000 acres (1,214 hectares); in some places it is 300 feet (91 meters) wide and 200 feet (61 meters) deep. This great gorge was eaten out of the landscape in only about 75 years. In addition to erosion damage, the practice of growing only one crop such as cotton or tobacco robbed the soil of much of its value.

However, many conservation programs are now being tried to restore small farms. Much work is being done to bring back the fertility of the soil, to keep erosion at a minimum, and to bring eroded land back to usefulness.

One novel Georgia program to help the farmer is the plan for farmers' markets operated by the Georgia Department of Agriculture. In these markets the farmers have a place to sell their crops, and the markets have been very successful in many locations such as Atlanta, Savannah, Thomasville, Columbus, Macon, Athens, and Augusta.

MADE IN GEORGIA

One of the world's best-known products originated in Georgia. Wherever anyone says, "Have a Coke," in whatever language around the globe, he pays tribute to an Atlanta druggist, John S. Pemberton, who originated the popular drink in 1886.

Georgia is among the leading states in the production of paper and paperboard. It is also high in the production of tire cord and the fabric used in automobile tires.

The textile industry is the state's oldest and largest, with a value of over a billion dollars per year. Among the smaller but notable activities in this field are the weavers of Rabun and the High Acres Mountain Guild weavers. Georgia has a special connection with another type of textile industry. In 1885 Mrs. Gertrude E. Whitener made the first tufted bedspread. Mrs. M.G. Cannon, Jr., of Dalton was able to sell tufted products to various New York department stores. Today, this is a multi-million-dollar business throughout the country annually.

The state receives annual income in the billions of dollars from its forests and woodlots. Georgia ranks first in the production of naval stores (turpentine and rosin). The pine trees are tapped, and the valuable fluids are drained out. From these come not only turpentine and rosin but also almost three hundred other products made from these basic materials. Hercules Naval Stores Plant at Brunswick is the largest of its kind in the country. The rosin taken from formerly useless tree stumps alone is made into more than two hundred products at Hercules. Valdosta is the world's largest naval stores market. The American Turpentine Farmers Association has its headquarters there.

One of Georgia's best-known early manufactured products was its famous Savannah grey brick, which the colonists began to make in 1733 in their first year in America. This is still a respected Georgia product.

The total annual value of Georgia's manfactured products was over eight billion dollars in the late 1970s.

"IN THEM THAR HILLS"

For centuries the Old World had looked upon the New World as a place where treasure could be found. The Aztecs and the Incas had their temples and idols of gold; the treasures of Mexico and Central and South America had provided wealth for the kings of Spain and Portugal. However, explorers had searched unsuccessfully for gold in the lands that are now the United States. In spite of tales about fabled cities of gold, the lands north of Mexico were a great disappointment.

Then, in the late 1820s, the cry of gold went up in northern Georgia, and Georgia became the first state in the United States where an important gold strike was made. Prospectors rushed into what is now Lumpkin County, and soon the region was filled with miners and panners; there were as many as fifteen thousand in a small area of the gold fields. A place called Licklog because of a hollow log filled with salt for cattle became the community of Dahlonega. The town had much of the rip-roaring atmosphere found later in the mining communities of the West.

Until the California gold rush of 1849, the Georgia gold fields and those of adjoining South Carolina provided most of the United States gold. A United States mint was set up at Dahlonega, and six million dollars in gold was coined there. Some gold is found in the region even today.

The most valuable minerals in Georgia are marble and granite. Today Georgia ranks high among the states in both granite and marble. Someone has called the Georgia reserves of these important stones "inexhaustible." Georgia marble has provided the beauty of its mottled coloring for many famous buildings, including the Field Museum in Chicago and St. Patrick's Cathedral, New York City. Some might say it is ironic that Georgia marble was used to form the world-renowned figure of Abraham Lincoln in the Lincoln Memorial at Washington. Others would feel that this represents the unity of the country Lincoln did so much to preserve.

Next in importance in Georgia mineral production are clay and clay products. Georgia ranks first among the states in kaolin clay. This is used for especially fine china and for filler and coating in what is known as "slick" paper, the kind used by magazines. In earlier days Georgia kaolin was shipped to England to be used in making the noted Wedgwood china. Today nearly all kaolin production in the United States comes from Georgia.

Georgia also ranks as the second state in producing fuller's earth and bauxite. Since bauxite is the raw material of aluminum, the importance of this mineral can easily be seen. Georgia is third in scrap mica and fourth in barite and feldspar.

The state also produces Portland cement, iron ore, limestone, sand and gravel, and talc. Moderate amounts of coal, flagstone, manganese, gold, peat, and other clays are mined. It is thought that other minerals such as copper, chromite, bentonite, corundum, olivine, tripoli, vermiculite, ilmenite, rutile, zircon, manazite sillimanite, and halloysite might be mined profitably. Geological investigations are revealing new mineral deposits, especially in south Georgia.

Altogether, Georgia minerals add about three hundred fifty million dollars to the annual income of the state.

TRANSPORTATION AND COMMUNICATION

Savannah is and always has been Georgia's leading port. Steamship lines operating out of Savannah number one hundred fourteen, and the state is still the nation's first-ranking cotton port. More than 6,000,000 tons (5,443,110 metric tons) of freight cleared the port of Savannah during 1964. Brunswick is the state's second-ranking seaport and the only other deepwater port in Georgia. It is also the headquarters of a picturesque fleet of Portuguese fishermen.

Development of several rivers has made ports for barge traffic at a number of important cities. The 199-mile (320-kilometer) deepening of the Savannah River converted Augusta into a port. In 1957 Bainbridge became operative as an inland port on the Flint River. Columbus is a major inland port on the Chattahoochee. This is as far as navigation can go at present on the river, but it is expected that Atlanta someday will be a seaport, with a 9-foot (2.7-meter) deep channel up the Chattahoochee.

The rivers were important even before the days of steam or diesel.

Many products were floated down the river in barges. Cotton often was sent in huge floating crates called "cotton boxes." When these reached the seaport, the crates were broken up for lumber. To encourage steamboats on the rivers, Georgia gave a monopoly in this field to Samuel Howard, who sent his steamboat *Enterprise* up the Savannah River in 1817. The monopoly caused high prices, and one ingenious man even built a boat with the paddlewheels turned by nineteen horses instead of steam. The United States Supreme Court broke the monopoly in 1824, and transportation moved ahead in Georgia. Such events as the historic voyage of the *Savannah* are especially noteworthy. In 1828 the Ogeechee Canal was opened to cut down costs of carrying freight between the Ogeechee and Savannah rivers.

In 1834 spectators flocked to the shipyards at Savannah to see a strange ship launched. Most of them said it would sink immediately; anyone with sense would know that a ship covered with iron would never float. However, it did float, and the *John Randolph* became the first ironclad ship in America.

Shrimp boats anchored in Brunswick harbor.

One of America's earliest forms of rail transportation was the horse-car road of Henry McAlpin. He began to use this in 1820 to carry his famous Savannah grey brick from the kilns to ships on the river. This "railroad" operated for forty-six years.

The first true railroad in Georgia was chartered in 1833, and the first trains began to run in 1837 over the 20 miles (32 kilometers) of track between Berzelia and Augusta. Today there are nearly 6,000 miles (9,656 kilometers) of railroad in Georgia.

Even more important today is the network of streets, roads, and highways totaling nearly 100,000 miles (160,934 kilometers). Georgia's first improvement on the Indian trails was a military road on St. Simons Island. By 1799 a stagecoach ran twice a week between Savannah and Augusta. One of the early "named" routes was the Jackson Trail, followed by General Jackson as he went into Florida to subdue the Indians.

Today Atlanta is one of the most important intersections of the interstate highway system and other essential roads. The addition of rail and airlines makes Atlanta the leading traffic and transportation center of the entire Southeast. Atlanta is second only to Chicago as an air transport center. The general headquarters of Delta Air Lines is in Atlanta.

Atlanta can also boast of a communications first. In 1922 the first two radio stations in the South began broadcasting in the city.

Georgia's first newspaper, the *Georgia Gazette,* was founded at Savannah in 1763. It did not continue until the present time. The oldest existing newspaper in the state, as well as all of the South, is the *Chronicle and Gazette* of Augusta, established in 1785. The *Columbus Messenger* was the first black daily to be published in the South. The nation's first Indian newspaper was the *Cherokee Phoenix,* first published at the Cherokee capital of New Echota in 1828. This appeared partly in the Cherokee language and partly in English.

Probably the most influential of the state's many daily newspapers and one of the country's leading papers is the *Atlanta Constitution,* begun in 1867. It has always had as its main interest its leadership in the establishment of a "new South."

Cason J. Callaway, an industrialist, created Callaway Gardens as a resort and recreational area. Callaway is also remembered for his programs for restoring unproductive Georgia farms.

Human Treasures

IN THE PUBLIC EYE

In 1848 Abraham Lincoln wrote, "I take up my pen to tell you that Mr. (Alexander H.) Stephens of Georgia, a little, slim, palefaced, consumptive man, with a voice like Logan's, has just completed the best speech of an hour's length I ever heard. My old, withered eyes are full of tears yet." Stephens was "slim" indeed, weighing only 90 pounds (40.8 kilograms), and also lame, but in spite of physical frailty, Alexander H. Stephens was one of the most unusual men this nation has produced. He was born in Taliaferro County. Ralph McGill wrote, "Friends helped him attend Franklin College (now the University of Georgia). . . He led his classes. Greek was a passion with him and he took the beauty and the precision of that language and its discipline into law, to the legislature, to the Federal Congress, and into the Confederacy. . . . " It was as a fellow congressman that Abraham Lincoln knew him.

Stephens opposed secession, but when it came in spite of him, he would not desert his friends, and eventually he was elevated to the vice-presidency of the Confederacy. He was arrested after the war and imprisoned for some months at Boston. In 1866 he was elected to the United States Senate but was not permitted to serve because of his former high position in the Confederate government.

He spent much of his later years in a wheelchair. His friends knew him as Little Aleck; remembering his early years, he helped many young people receive an education and was noted for his kindness as well as his generosity. Little Aleck returned to politics and was elected governor, but the strain was too great on his feeble health, and he died in 1883.

As a Union prisoner he had written, "Let my last breath be my native air. My native land, my country, the only one that is country to me, is Georgia." He was buried on the grounds of his estate, Liberty Hall, in Crawfordville.

Prominent in the same period as Stephens was wartime governor of Georgia, Joseph E. Brown, who served longer than any other chief executive of the state. He was one of the most controversial figures of his time as well as one of the most combative. He quarreled bitterly with Confederate President Jefferson Davis. Brown felt that the individual states should have the right to raise and manage their own troops, and Davis disagreed. Brown defied the Southern president and said that Davis was as great an "enemy of the South" as Lincoln.

Another prominent Georgia figure in the Confederate period was General Robert Toombs. He helped write the Compromise of 1850, which was supposed to keep the nation from war. When that war came, Toombs served first as secretary of state for the Confederacy, and then served in the army. At the war's close he was hidden in the famous Prather House near Toccoa until he was able to escape to Europe. He returned to the United States, but he never took the oath of allegiance to the United States that was required of former Confederate officials. For this reason he has been known as the "unreconstructed rebel."

Benjamin Harvey Hill was another who opposed secession but was loyal to the South when it came. After the war he advised his fellow Georgians to accept defeat and do the best they could, which made him hated by many. However, he was elected to Congress from Georgia and later to the Senate. It is said that he was one of the most influential of all those who tried to persuade President Hayes to remove federal troops from Georgia.

Secretary of state under Presidents Kennedy and Johnson, Dean Rusk is a native of Georgia.

An earlier Georgia man of national fame was Button Gwinnett, one of Georgia's signers of the Declaration of Independence. He was killed in a duel with Lachlan McIntosh over a political argument. Another Georgia figure connected with a political document was William H. Crawford of Lexington. He is said to have had a large part in helping President James Monroe formulate what we know today as the Monroe Doctrine.

A later politician of great power for more than twenty-five years was Thomas E. Watson of Thomson. He ran for vice-president and later for president on the Populist Party ticket. His death in 1920 came during his term as a United States senator. Hoke Smith, lawyer, newspaper publisher, United States secretary of the interior, governor, and United States senator was one of a number of dynamic leaders who directed political reforms in an attempt to solve some of the social and economic problems of beginning industrialization.

Another Georgia senator has a unique distinction in American history. This was Mrs. Rebecca Felton of Cartersville. When she was appointed to the Senate after the death of Senator Watson, she became the first woman ever to serve as a United States senator.

The Reverend Joseph R. Wilson was pastor of the First Presbyterian Church of Augusta, and so it was that the manse of that church became the boyhood home of a president of the United States—Joseph's son, Thomas Woodrow Wilson. As a young man, on a visit to Rome, Wilson met Ellen Axson, and they were married later in Savannah. The first Mrs. Wilson is buried in Myrtle Hill Cemetery in Rome.

Another president of the United States had a more famous association with Georgia. Franklin Delano Roosevelt had been assistant secretary of the navy under Woodrow Wilson and was an unsuccessful candidate for vice-president in 1920. Most people thought that his career was over when he was severely crippled by polio in 1921. Roosevelt gave much credit to the benefits of Warm Springs for the partial recovery of his health.

When F.D. Roosevelt became president, his association with Warm Springs was one of the best-known aspects of his life. He built a small home at Warm Springs and visited there whenever he could to escape some of the cares of office. His journey to the international conference at Yalta had almost exhausted him. As soon as he could he went to Warm Springs for a rest.

Posing for a portrait being painted by Madame Elizabeth Shoumatoff, he suddenly complained of a terrible headache, soon became unconscious, and died very shortly of a stroke. The attention of the world centered on the small house in Warm Springs. When the body of the president was carried in state through Warm Springs to the railroad station for the last journey back to Washington, it passed the silent watchers who were his neighbors and friends. Many had been helped by him to overcome their paralysis.

MR. PRESIDENT

The only native Georgian to become president is former governor James Earl Carter, Jr., who took office in 1977.

DISCOVERERS

A milestone in man's age-long struggle for life occurred in Georgia. Dr. Crawford W. Long was practicing at Jefferson when a Mr. James V. Venable asked him to remove two small tumors from his neck. Dr. Long himself described what happened: "... I mentioned to him ... that the operation might be performed without pain, and proposed operating on him while under the influence of ether. He consented.... The ether was given to Mr. Venable on a towel, and when fully under its influence, I extirpated the tumor...."

In this way Dr. Long became the first surgeon to use ether as an anesthetic. Dr. Long and Alexander H. Stephens are the Georgia representatives in the national hall of fame, Statuary Hall, in the Capitol at Washington.

Another distinguished Georgia physician and surgeon was Dr. Robert Battey of Rome. One of the operations he developed is now known by his name in medical circles throughout the world.

One of the most far-reaching events in the history of invention occurred in Georgia almost as an accident. Eli Whitney graduated from Yale and thought he had an appointment to tutor in a wealthy family of Savannah, but when he reached the city, the position was already filled. He had met Mrs. Nathanael Greene, widow of the general, and she invited him to visit her estate, Mulberry Grove. During a conversation with some friends of Mrs. Greene, one of them said, "The man who can invent a machine to separate the lint of cotton from the seed will make a fortune." Mrs. Greene turned to

Whitney and said, "Anyone who can fix a watch as you fixed mine has the ability to create any type of machine; you are that man."

Inspired by such confidence, Whitney set up a small workshop at Mulberry Grove, made his own tools and spent the winter working. The machine he made had a roller that pulled the cotton through a slotted metal plate and separated the seeds, but he had not yet found a way of keeping the lint from clinging to the roller. According to some accounts, Mrs. Greene went to her dressing table, came back with a brush and held it against the plate as the roller turned. The first successful cotton gin was placed in operation at Washington, Georgia, by Whitney. He had perfected the device while working on the plantation belonging to Phineas Miller, who had become the partner of Whitney. Almost everyone agrees that this single invention changed the whole economy of the country by making cotton a material which could be inexpensively worked into fabric.

Another Georgia man, Lancelot Johnson of Madison, also was important in the cotton industry. At one time the seeds of cotton were only a nuisance. In 1834 Johnson discovered a way of crushing the seeds and making an oil from them. Today cottonseed oil and the livestock feed from seed pulp are worth hundreds of millions per year in the United States.

Still another advance in cotton production was made by a Georgia firm. The Lummus Cotton Gin Company installed an air blast to help in the removal of cotton seeds. This is considered to be the most important improvement in the field since Eli Whitney's time.

Other Georgia inventors were Dr. Francis Goulding, Joseph Eve, and William Longstreet. Dr. Goulding invented the first sewing machine. However, his machine had some flaws which required perfecting by others, such as Elias Howe. Eve had many patents on steam-powered equipment and was also active in chemical work. As early as 1807 William Longstreet had built a steamboat that moved along the Savannah River at 5 miles (8 kilometers) per hour. Just as he was about to apply for a patent, word came to him of the successful and much publicized success of Robert Fulton's steamboat work in New York, and he dropped his patent application.

The Rumph family of Marshallville was noted for its triumphs in horticulture. Samuel H. Rumph developed the famed Elberta peach, named for his wife Elberta. Their son, Lewis A. Rumph, developed the luscious peach which he named the Georgia Belle in honor of Mrs. Belle Hall. These peaches have become standards in the peach industry.

Other noted horticulturists were Julius Berckmans of Augusta and John Couper, whose plantation on Sea Island was developed into what has been called the country's "first agricultural experiment station." Couper raised almost every plant that could grow in his climate. He was especially successful in growing olives and producing olive oil.

Eliza Frances Andrews gained distinction as the first woman ever elected to the International Academy of Science.

CREATIVE GEORGIANS

One of the most popular books of all times was the product of a Georgia author and had its setting in Georgia during the war between the states. Unsuccessful authors take hope from the success story of Margaret Mitchell of Atlanta, who had written a huge novel about the war, which was not published for a long period. The book, of course, was *Gone With the Wind,* which won the Pulitzer Prize in 1937, and also went on to become one of the most successful motion pictures of all time.

Another Georgia Pulitzer Prize winner was Caroline Miller of Baxley. Her novel of Georgia during the Revolutionary War, *Lamb in His Bosom,* was given the award in 1934. Another woman, Corra Harris, was the first novelist in Georgia to win a nationwide reputation for her work. Yet another popular Georgia woman novelist was Augusta Evans Wilson, author of the well-liked work *Saint Elmo.*

Sidney Lanier, born in Macon, has been called "Georgia's most celebrated poet." Another George poet, Thomas Holley Chivers, a friend of Edgar Allan Poe, once accused Poe of copying his work. Chivers' biographer says of him "...Chivers also tried to build poems out of pure sound, with results that are surprisingly modern."

66

Other well-known poets are Conrad Aiken and Frank L. Stanton.

Flannery O'Connor, of Savannah, was a notable novelist. She had poor health and died at age thirty-nine in 1964.

"Georgia's Aesop" is the nickname given to one of the best-known writers of Georgia—Joel Chandler Harris, born near Eatonton, creator of the *Uncle Remus* stories and tales of *Br'er Rabbit*. He was the first writer to use black dialect to a great extent. The Chandler home in Atlanta was known as the Wren's Nest, because when a wren built a nest in his mailbox, the author built another mailbox in order not to disturb the mother-to-be.

Two other widely contrasting Georgia writers are the sensitive children's author of *Young Marooners* and *Marooners Island,* Francis R. Goulding, and the earthy Erskine Caldwell, author of *Tobacco Road* and other books.

Juliette Gordon Low, described as a "peppery" sculptress, gained fame not only for her artwork but as the founder of the Girl Scouts of America. Edward Greene Malbone was one of the best-known painters of miniatures. Edward Kemeys, born in Savannah, is perhaps most noted for the fifty bronzes of "Wild Animals of North America," displayed in an honored place in the National Gallery of Art in the nation's capital.

Br'er Rabbit,
created by Joel Chandler Harris.

Roland Hayes, renowned singer and composer, was born near Carryville. Lowell Mason was the composer of the hymns "Nearer, My God, to Thee" and "My Faith Looks Up to Thee." Another well-loved song, "Mighty Lak a Rose" was the work of Frank L. Stanton, sometimes called Georgia's "poet laureate."

SUCH INTERESTING PEOPLE

Two of the best-known personalities of history were among the earliest settlers of the Georgia colony. These were the brothers John and Charles Wesley. Charles served as General Oglethorpe's secretary; he preached in Christ Church at Frederica on St. Simons Island. After about six months in which he was very unhappy, Charles Wesley had what has been called a "historic quarrel" with Oglethorpe, and he returned to England.

His brother John preached at Savannah, founded what is frequently recognized as the first Protestant Sunday school and did missionary work among the Indians and greatly aided a group of Moravian settlers. He, too, became discouraged in the New World and returned home to England where he gained fame as the founder of Methodism. Possibly he was hastened in returning when his sweetheart, Sophia Hopkey, eloped to South Carolina with another man.

Better-known Georgia women include Alice McLellan Birney of Marietta, founder of the National Congress of Parents and Teachers; Moina Michael of Athens and Monroe, who originated the national custom of the veterans' poppy day; Joanna Troutman of Knoxville, who created the Lone Star flag of Texas; and Sarah Hillhouse, first woman in America to own and edit a newspaper.

Also prominent in the editorial field was Henry Woodfin Grady, "directing genius" of the Atlanta *Constitution,* who gained national fame for his "Vision of the New South."

Prominent in business were Asa G. Candler, who built the giant Coca-Cola Company after buying it from the founder, Lazarus Straus (who began as a peddler, opened a store in Talbotton, and later became the owner of the giant Macys department store in New York City), and Cason J. Callaway. Callaway, an industrialist, is also noted for his programs in restoring unproductive Georgia farms and for his renowned Callaway Gardens. R. S. Abbot of St. Simons gained wealth as the successful publisher of one of the country's best-known black daily newspapers, the *Chicago Defender*.

The civil rights leader, Reverend Martin Luther King, Jr., was born in Atlanta in 1929. As a Baptist minister, he preached non-violence. His famous "I have a dream" speech was given in Washington, D.C. in 1963. Reverend King helped begin the Southern Christian Leadership Conference. He is buried near Ebanezer Baptist Church in Atlanta.

Among Georgia's patriot-heroes are Lieutenant Thomas M. Brumby of Marietta, who represented the navy in the surrender of Manila in 1898 and first raised the United States flag over the city walls, and Bishop Leonidas Polk, known as the "Fighting Bishop of the Confederacy," who died in the Battle of Pine Mountain. A Revolutionary hero, General Elijah Clarke, had a career with a strange turn. After the war he seized Indian lands and with his followers set up what he called an independent country—the Trans-Oconee Republic. This was put down by the Georgia governor on orders from President George Washington.

Georgia also has its heroes in the field of sports. One of the nation's most beloved sports figures is sometimes called "the greatest golfer of all time." This is Robert Tyre Jones, Jr., better known as Bobby Jones. In later years he has been prominently associated with Augusta's National Golf Course, where the famed Masters' Tournament is held each year. One of the best-known baseball players of all time was Tyrus Raymond (Ty) Cobb, also of Augusta. Cobb won more batting championships than anyone else in baseball history. He also holds the record for the most base hits (4,191), and most runs scored (2,244).

One of the most notable of the Indian people was George Gist, known as Sequoya, who came to Georgia and spent some years there. He is best known for his invention of the Cherokee alphabet and the system of Cherokee writing.

*Brooks Hall, on the University of Georgia campus,
houses the College of Business Administration. It
is named for Dr. R. Preston Brooks, former business
professor and dean of faculties at the university.*

Teaching and Learning

Georgia has achieved a number of distinctions in education. Wesleyan College of Macon is claimed to be the first college in the world chartered to grant degrees to women. Its charter was granted in 1836. The University of Georgia is said to be the first of all state universities to receive a charter.

The state university was chartered in 1785 after 40,000 acres (16,187 hectares) of land had been set aside in 1783 to endow such a university. John Milledge donated 633 acres (256 hectares) of land for the university and it opened in 1801 at Athens. The first permanent building was finished in 1805. Other state institutions were established over the years. In 1931 seventeen of these were placed under the control of a State Board of Regents in a single system of state colleges and universities. Georgia was one of the earlier states to do this, and most of the other states have since followed this lead.

The Peabody School of Forestry of the university, founded in 1906, was the first of its kind in the South. The university's School of Agriculture is especially outstanding, as is its Lumpkin Law School, which became part of the university in 1859. The Medical College of Georgia, another branch of the university, is at Augusta.

Among recent additions to the Georgia state university system is Armstrong State College, formerly a junior college.

One of the world's best-known and most highly rated technical schools is Georgia Institute of Technology on the edge of downtown Atlanta, better known as "Georgia Tech," home of the "Ramblin' Wreck" made famous in the song. Georgia Tech is especially renowned for its W. Harrison Hightower Building, said to be the most complete textile study center in the country.

Atlanta is one of the great educational centers. In addition to Georgia Tech there are 25 other universities, colleges, and institutions of advanced study in the Atlanta area. One of these is a group of colleges associated with Atlanta University; these include Spelman, Morehouse, Clark, and Morris Brown colleges and the Interdenominational Theological Center. Oglethorpe University and Emory University are other fine schools of the Atlanta area. Emory was begun with a gift of one million dollars from Asa G. Candler, Sr., and five hundred thousand dollars from the city of Atlanta. Rockefeller Hall at Morehouse College was built with what is said to be the first contribution to any college ever made by John D. Rockefeller, Sr.

Some of the other Georgia institutions include Shorter College, Rome; Valdosta State College, Valdosta; Wesleyan College, Macon; Piedmont College, Demorest; Paine College, Augusta; Agnes Scott College, Decatur; Brenau College, Gainesville; and LaGrange College, La Grange. Mercer University, Macon, was begun as a manual labor school, where boys worked to pay for their schooling.

As early as 1568 Brother Domingo Augustine taught the Yamassee Indians at the Spanish mission on St. Catherines Island. The first school of the English period was Irene, established in 1735. The Bethesda Mission established in 1740 by George Whitefield and James Habersham is the oldest orphanage in America still in operation. As early as 1743 Savannah and Augusta opened free schools.

Georgia claims to be the first colony to establish a free high school—Richmond Academy, founded at Augusta in 1783.

A remarkable philosophy of education was expressed by Abraham Baldwin, who said, "As it is the distinguishing happiness of free government that civil order should be the result of choice and not of necessity, and the common wishes of the people become the law of the land, their public prosperity and even existence, very much depends upon suitably forming the minds and morals of their citizens."

Julien Froumontaine opened a school for blacks in 1818. The Augusta Free School Society was founded in 1821. In 1837 a plan for common schools by Alexander H. Stephens was adopted. By the mid-1850s there were about three thousand "Old Field Schools" in Georgia; these were a type of private rural school.

Two currently prevailing educational ideas originated in Georgia; these were the Parent-Teacher Association, started at Marietta, and the world's first sororities, begun in 1851 at Wesleyan College, Macon.

One of Georgia's interesting private schools is Riverside Military Academy at Gainesville. Each year the whole student body and faculty move to Florida for the winter.

Among the most unusual schools anywhere are the Berry Schools south of Summerville, founded by Miss Martha Berry. She began her teaching by telling Bible stories to her father's tenants' children, and became known as the "Sunday Lady." She also operated a day school for adults in the old mountain church. She soon was riding about through the country teaching children and helping organize classes for sewing. With her sister, Frances, and Miss Elizabeth Brewster, Martha Berry organized a school in a log cabin on her 300-acre (121-hectare) farm. With five boys as students, her first boarding school opened in 1902. After she had used all her funds, she began asking for funds from wealthy persons and received much help in her work.

As she continued her educational work, Miss Berry's reputation grew until she was recognized as one of the leading educators. In 1931 she was named one of twelve outstanding women of America. Although Martha Berry died in 1942, her educational work is still being carried on.

A symbol of Barry College, the old mill wheel.

73

Toccoa Falls

Enchantment of Georgia

Georgia relishes its nickname of "Empire State of the South." Such a title is appropriate to the transportation, manufacturing, and marketing hub of the Deep South. However, the charm of the South as symbolized by Greek porticos, Doric columns, and romantic traditions is still found. Here is a land where modern fortresses (air force bases) are not far from communities where sacred harp singing is still carried on, or from a region where the mountain people hold their traditional foxhunts.

Here also is a land of 3,000 square miles (7,770 square kilometers) of forested mountains, deep lakes, and clear mountain streams, contrasted with miles of sunny beaches and sun-drenched isles, with still further contrast in the misty swamps where alligators splash and exotic tropical birds preen their elaborate plumage.

WHERE IT ALL BEGAN; SAVANNAH

Some who know Savannah well have described it as "America's most beautiful city." Savannah was planned around its "twenty-four jewels"—squares or parks, "little green acres that transform Savannah." As someone has said, the "squares are the signature of Savannah," just as in the early days they were laid out as rallying points against possible Indian attacks.

The walk down Bull Street, with its five squares plus Forsyth Park, is "one of the most historic walks of America." The street was named for General Oglethorpe's assistant William Bull. The square just south of Bay Street is Johnson Square, the first of the squares to be laid out. Johnson Square is named for South Carolina Governor Robert Johnson, friend and helper of Oglethorpe. Revolutionary War hero Nathanael Greene and his son are buried there and remembered with an imposing monument. The colonists came to Johnson Square to find the time of day on a sundial. There is still a sundial in the square, replacing the original one.

In the center of Chippewa Square is the statue of James Edward

Oglethorpe, Georgia's respected founder. The statue is Savannah's only work by the dean of American sculptors, Daniel Chester French, and was erected by patriotic societies in 1910.

The most historic part of the city is Yamacraw Bluff, where the colonists and their leader were greeted by wise old Chief Tomochichi. The present City Hall is near the place where they camped for the first night, and a marble bench on the grass plot beyond City Hall marks the spot where Oglethorpe pitched his tent that night. Behind City Hall was the dock from which the S. S. *Savannah* set forth on her historic voyage.

Nearby is Factors Walk. It took its name from the business houses and offices of the cotton factors whose buildings were connected by a strange and picturesque network of iron and concrete bridgeways and cobblestone walk, the latter built of stones brought in ships as ballast. Visitors may still wander over these unique walkways. The names of long-gone cotton merchants may still be made out on some of the buildings. Here King Cotton had his mythical throne and ruled the whole world of textiles for a time.

The Cotton Exchange building was built over Drayton Street. This was done because the city council in 1887 had passed an ordinance requiring the street to be kept open. "Air rights" were granted for the building to be made above the street. This is believed to be the country's first building built on air rights—now a common practice. The Cotton Exchange is presently the headquarters of the city's Chamber of Commerce. Visitors may still see the word C O T T O N spelled out in the fine old stained-glass windows.

Another of the landmarks on the bluff is the quaint old harbor light erected in 1858 as a beacon for ships.

The Trustees Gardens, where Oglethorpe, Wesley, and others loved to walk amid the quiet beauty, fell into decay until 1945. Then Mrs. H. Hansell Hillyer had the inspiration to restore the gardens. Today it is one of the most popular areas of the city. There is now a famous restaurant in the old Pirates' House in the Trustees Gardens. Some of the action of *Treasure Island* by Robert Louis Stevenson is said to have taken place in the Pirates' House. It is claimed that old Cap'n Flint, who buried the fabulous treasure on Treasure Island, died there in an upstairs room, shouting, "Darby, fetch aft the rum!" and the ghost of the villainous captain is said even yet to haunt the Pirates' House on moonless nights.

Many a man drinking in the Pirates' House inn in the old days was drugged, carried unconscious through a legendary secret tunnel, and shanghaied for the crew of a waiting ship in the river. Legend tells of a Savannah policeman who stopped for a drink and awoke on a four-masted schooner sailing for China. It took him two years to make his way back to Savannah.

Savannah is a city of many fine houses. Among the most notable of these is the Davenport House, which is one of the great Georgian houses of America. It was built in 1815 by master builder Isaiah Davenport and is furnished with priceless relics of the Davenport family. It is now the headquarters of Historic Savannah Foundation, Inc.

The Owens-Thomas House, designed by a twenty-three-year-old prodigy, architect William Jay, is thought of as "one of the finest in America—a perfect example of Regency architecture in America." Another prominent house open to the public is the Juliette Gordon Low house, birthplace of the founder of the Girl Scouts of America.

One of the largest churches in the Southeast is the Cathedral of St. John the Baptist, finished in 1876 and restored in 1898 after a fire. Christ Episcopal Church, first church in Georgia, was founded by the original colonists in 1733. Its first ministers were John and Charles Wesley. Temple Mickve Israel was erected in 1876. It is the third oldest Jewish congregation in the United States, also dating back to 1733.

Fort Pulaski has been called "Savannah's most spectacular structure." Located on Cockspur Island, it is now a national monument. The fort took twenty-five years and twenty-five million bricks to build. Where nails were used, the heads were covered with Georgia pine so that sparks would not be struck on them to set off the gunpowder. Fort Frederica is now also a national monument, and historic Fort McAllister near Richmond Hill has been restored as a museum of earlier warfare. Its earthen walls held out long after the supposedly impregnable walls of Fort Pulaski had given in.

The Juliette Gordon Low house is now a scouting shrine.

One of the country's outstanding small art galleries is Telfair Academy of Arts and Sciences, the oldest museum of art in the entire Southeast. It is housed in the old Telfair mansion, given to the city by Miss Mary Telfair in 1875. A unique museum designed especially for young people is the Youth Museum of Savannah, with animal groups, live animals, science and industry exhibits, and a planetarium.

A cotton warehouse of 1755 in the Factors Walk area has been converted into the Factors Walk Military Museum, emphasizing exhibits of the war between the states. A unique Savannah museum project is that of banker Mills Lane who brought the sailing ship *Cruz del Sur* to Savannah harbor. The ship and nearby space in the Artley Building are used as a Savannah Maritime Museum.

A rapidly growing cultural organization of Savannah is the Savannah Symphony, organized in 1953.

GEORGIA'S SOUTHERN THIRD

Georgia's coast is decorated with golden islands, like gems on a necklace threaded by the important Intercoastal Waterway. To Georgians and vacationers everywhere the islands have such magic names as Jekyll, Sapelo, St. Simons, and Cumberland. Jekyll Island

78

once was owned by an exclusive club of millionaires. Now it is a beautiful state park. Blackbeard's Island has become a national wildlife refuge.

Darien is known for its magnificent General Oglethorpe Oak. At Darien are many good examples of "tabby" buildings. This kind of construction, formed with a mortar of oyster shell, has been used on the Georgia coast since the time of the Spaniards. The most impressive ruins of tabby architecture on the coast are those of the old Spanish Santa Maria Mission near Kingsland.

Probably few regions anywhere have as great a reputation for mystery as Owaquaphenoga. This Indian word means trembling earth and it gives us the word Okefenokee. Much of the land in Okefenokee Swamp really does tremble. Gases raise masses of roots and sediment to the surface; there they collect dirt and other debris and turn into floating islands. Sometimes they become large and drift to land, but often they still "tremble" on an uncertain base. This great wonderland of black water and jungle-like growth dotted with sunny savannahs is now the Okefenokee National Wildlife Refuge. In some parts of this eerie region, only those who know the area well dare to venture into the brooding swamp. Strangers become hopelessly lost. The hooting of owls, the fluttering wings of the innumerable birds, the bellow of alligators, and other sounds combine in a kind of muted roar known locally as the "booming of the swamp."

The visitor may stroll out on elevated, railed cypress boardwalks and view this fantastic wonderland, where snow-white and buttery-gold water lilies float on an ebony mirror of dark water—where bright green cypress trees draped with ghostly gray moss sway in the soft swamp breeze.

Dark, mysterious water lanes knife through the thick cypress jungle into a world of strange, forbidding shadows, dappled with patches of soft yellow sunshine. A bullfrog croaks throatily from a mossy fallen cypress log. Huge billowing jade ferns thrust out of the black water, almost obscuring the giant alligator cradled in their midst.

From the 75-foot (23-meter) high observation tower, visitors have a view across the cypress crowns, and the great swamp stretches for miles in majestic panorama of vast freshwater marshes, forested islands, and pure dark-water lakes. Overhead a hawk circles slowly in the blue sky. Yellow-brown swamp grass ripples in the wind. Below, a flock of white heron wades in a black pool, casting shadows on the ebony water. A big bass leaps clear of the water and slaps back in, shattering the water mirror.

Here is a region that is one of nature's most interesting and unusual masterpieces; man has tried with little success to "reclaim" it, and with the help of those who value natural wilderness areas, Okefenokee, one of the most beautiful and fantastic landscapes in the world, may be saved for future generations.

Okefenokee Swamp Park has a serpentarium and wildlife museum where many swamp creatures may be observed. The otter pool is a favorite with many. Daily wildlife lectures are scheduled. The story of the Okefenokee is also the story of the friendly unaffected people who live in and around it.

One of the government preserves in the area is Stephen C. Foster State Park, where the Suwannee River, made famous by Foster, begins its murky course.

Traveling inland from the coast in southern Georgia, the visitor notes three unique features of the landscape. Mile after mile is traveled through long-leaf and slash pine forest, often carpeted with undergrowth of palmetto or gall-berry bushes. Only on sandy ridges near streams and in stream basins are oak, maple, and other hardwood trees seen. In clearings of occasional cultivated areas, the tall tobacco barn appears time after time. Occasionally the long, low, and narrow chicken house beside the farm dwelling can be seen. This is usually new, with its sides covered with plastic.

Since the numerous ponds and streams are always nearby, it is a common sight to see a boat at many dwellings, often parked in the carport.

Thomasville is known as "The City of Roses"; here even the telephone poles are covered with climbing roses. In the Thomasville area sprawl the great estates built by people from the North as winter homes.

80

The Lapham-Patterson House, in Thomasville, has been restored.

Tifton is one of the principal United States tobacco markets. A tobacco auction is also held at Valdosta. A point of interest in Valdosta is The Crescent, a house built in a semi-circle traced on the ground by its owner's walking stick.

Cordele calls itself the "Watermelon Capital of the World," and it holds an annual watermelon festival to celebrate this position. Radium Springs is a popular resort, with its spring flowing at the rate of 70,000 gallons (264,979 liters) per minute. Albany is at the head of navigation on the Flint River. It has an interesting junior museum. Cairo is the country's largest center for the production of pure cane syrup. Providence Caverns near Lumpkin were formed by erosion into canyons resembling those of the West, with delicate colors and a kind of beauty.

Douglas and Moultrie are important agricultural marketing and processing centers. Both are rapidly diversifying their economies, however. Douglas is becoming an important mobile homes production center.

THE MIDDLE THIRD

Augusta was the second town laid out by General Oglethorpe for settlement in Georgia. The town grew about old Fort Augusta; the waters of the fall line made it an important place for early mills. An 1845 account describes the city— "... There are in the country some 20 sawmills, and the same number of gristmills. There are stone quarries in several directions; machine shops for railroad cars, and for almost every kind of machinery, are in operation, which gives the place a businesslike appearance. Flouring mills are splendid." Later Augusta became a leading tobacco market.

Augusta is the world's unofficial winter golf capital. Its Masters Invitation Tournament is one of the top golf competitions anywhere. Many golfers call the Augusta Golf Course the most beautiful in the world. With the help of Bobby Jones it was built on the horticultural gardens of Prosper Julius Berckmans. Each hole has its own name, such as number 5, Magnolia, and number 10, Camellia. Augusta's best-known amateur golfer was President Dwight D. Eisenhower, who had a vacation White House built near the club.

Another building known as the White House is the restored inn, the oldest house in Augusta; this is considered Georgia's most important existing Revolutionary shrine. The Signers' Monument, dedicated to Georgia's three signers of the Declaration of Independence, the Confederate Monument, and the Poet's Monument are prominent memorials in Augusta.

Augusta Museum and Gertrude Herbert Memorial Institute of Art are important cultural institutions. The Municipal Auditorium is interesting because it can be reduced from a 5,054 seat hall to a music hall seating 1,000.

Milledgeville, laid out in 1803 and named for John Milledge, then governor, is one of America's few cities planned specifically as a capital. The city served as Georgia's capital for sixty-one years. There are more than sixty homes and buildings in Milledgeville of historical interest.

Indian Springs State Park is sometimes called the oldest state park in the country. The Creek Indians once gathered there to take advantage of the mineral waters. At the park is the thirty-five-room house of Creek Indian Chief William McIntosh, who was forced out by the settlers and then murdered by his own discontented kinsmen. Nearby is the great Oconee National Forest.

Macon began as a trading post and then was a fort during the War of 1812. It is in the middle of the state and today is the marketing center for the Georgia peach industry. Sidney Lanier lived in Macon, practicing law until he turned to poetry. His bust in the Macon Memorial Library is by sculptor Gutzon Borglum. Another outstanding Macon institution is the Museum of Arts and Sciences and Planetarium. Near Macon is Ocmulgee National Monument, site of some of the finest prehistoric finds in the country.

Andersonville is the location of Andersonville National Cemetery and Military Prison Park. The prison was built to hold 10,000 men, and at one time it held 33,000 northern military prisoners. The suffering was great. Of the total 49,485 prisoners held, 12,462 prisoners died at Andersonville. In the National Cemetery are graves of 14,300 Union soldiers and other military dead.

Power from the falls of the Chattahoochee helped make Columbus the second-most important manufacturing city of the Confederacy. The Eagle and Phenix Mill at Columbus is said to be the first mill to use hydroelectric power for lighting. On display at the Confederate Naval Museum is the Confederate Ironclad *Muscogee,* launched in 1864 but never in action. Another Columbus museum is the Museum of Arts and Crafts. Nearby Fort Benning is considered to be America's largest and most complete military post.

Instant fame came to a small community between Columbus and Albany, when its best-known resident began to campaign for the presidency of the United States. When Jimmy Carter gained that exalted post, his home town of Plains had already become internationally renowned.

Near Warm Springs is Franklin D. Roosevelt State Park. Here is the Little White House built by the president and preserved as a museum in his memory.

Near Pine Mountain are the Callaway Gardens, a most complete resort and recreational area.

THE NORTHERN THIRD

Washington was the first city in the country to be incorporated honoring George Washington's name. Here the Confederate cabinet held its last meeting. Memorabilia of the Confederacy are displayed at the Washington-Wilkes Confederate Museum. There is a legend that the Confederate gold not captured by Northern troops is still buried in the Washington region.

Other Confederate memories are strong at Crawfordville. Here is Liberty Hall, home of Confederate Vice-president Alexander H. Stephens, in what is now Stephens Memorial State Park. The statesman is buried near his home.

Athens was named in honor of the Greek center of culture and the city has been determined to live up to its name. Georgia's classic city receives an immense boost through the University of Georgia. Features of the university are a Science Center of six buildings, a forestry preserve, chapel, historic buildings, Georgia Museum of Art, and the Georgia Center for Continuing Education. This facility is host to hundreds of conventions each year and has an auditorium similar to that of the United Nations. A prized possession of the university is the original draft of the constitution of the Confederate States of America—written in longhand.

One of Athens' strangest attractions is the "tree that owns itself," standing on a plot that was deeded in the tree's own name. A far greater distinction is the fact that Athens was the home of the first garden club in America. The Founders Memorial Garden is maintained in memory of this beginning.

Gainesville, on the shores of Lake Lanier, is a gateway to the great mountain region of Georgia—in some places a primitive wilderness, made even more beautiful in season by wild azalea, rhododendron, dogwood, redbud, and mountain laurel. In Georgia is the southern end of the Appalachian Trail, which reaches to Maine. The trail winds for 100 miles (161 kilometers) through Georgia's mountain fastnesses. Highlights of the mountain area include Toccoa ("beautiful" in Cherokee) Falls, surrounded by park lands with 486 varieties of plants; Tallulah Falls and Gorge; 729-foot (222-meter)

Amicalola Falls near Dawsonville, its Indian name meaning tumbling water; 400-foot (122-meter) high De Soto Falls; and Cane Creek Falls. Stone Pile Gap marks the grave of Indian Princess Trahlyta. Passersby place stones on her grave for luck.

Dahlonega, heart of Georgia's gold rush, is now noted for its Pioneer Gold Museum. Through the mud floor of the museum building runs a small stream, where visitors may pan for gold. Many gold operations are demonstrated in the museum, operated by the Chamber of Commerce. After a heavy rain, tiny gold particles may sometimes still be picked up on Dahlonega streets. The dome of the state capitol gleams with a gold leaf surface contributed by the people of Dahlonega.

Bulloch Hall, Roswell, was the scene of the marriage of Theodore Roosevelt's parents. At Marietta is another national cemetery, the burial place of 10,158 Union soldiers. The region of the Battle of Kennesaw Mountain is now a national battlefield park. There Union troops lost over 3,000 men as against 808 for the Confederate forces. There is a visitors' center with a museum at the park. George Washington Carver State Park near Acworth was established in recognition of the scientist. Another memorial, Friendship Monument at Cartersville, was put up by Mark A. Cooper as a tribute to almost forty friends and creditors who helped him out of a tight financial situation.

A very remarkable restoration almost manages to bring to life once more the Cherokee capital of New Echota, northeast of Calhoun. At Calhoun is a statue of the remarkable Indian savant Sequoya. Another unusual Indian leader was Chief Joseph Vann. His mansion between Dalton and Chatsworth, once the showcase of the Cherokee Nation, has been restored. It is notable for its secret passage and "floating" stairway.

Chickamauga and Chattanooga National Military Park, founded in 1890, is the oldest and largest of all our national military parks. Those who visit the park are impressed with how much the now quiet park seems to come alive with the tragedies of that terrible two-day battle of Chickamauga, which turned into one of the greatest Confederate triumphs.

It has been said that seven hills, five men, three rivers, and a hat all took part in the founding of Rome. The region's seven hills, like those of ancient Rome, inspired the five founders of the community to put the name Rome among others in the hat, and the name that was drawn, by chance, was Rome.

Carrollton is world-renowned for what its people have accomplished through cooperation. Their work has been labeled "the most interesting example of community organization and planning in the state." Among the many accomplishments of the people of Carrollton was the creation of a sizeable lake by a group of citizens without any government assistance.

CAPITAL AND LARGEST CITY; ATLANTA

The first recorded mention of the Atlanta area was made in 1782. In 1813 the first European settlement was begun as a fort; until this time the site had been occupied by the Cherokee village of Standing Peachtree. The community grew as a railroad town until it had a population of about 20,000 in 1861. During the early years of the Civil War the city escaped battle, although as many as 80,000 wounded officers were hospitalized in Atlanta.

However, when Sherman began his siege, citizens took refuge in trenches in their backyards from the Union artillery fire, and there was terrible suffering. Those who could, escaped to the south. After the war the city seemed to thrive. By 1866 the population of Atlanta was almost twice the size it had been before Sherman attacked. There was a lively struggle with Milledgeville for the capital.

In 1883 the legislature appropriated a million dollars for a new capitol. The great gold-domed building was modeled after the national Capitol at Washington. Georgia marble was used for the beautiful interior finish of walls, floors, and steps. The building was dedicated on July 4, 1889. According to Ben W. Fortson, "The epic accomplishment of erecting this magnificent capitol within the appropriation of $1,000,000 and having $118.43 left in the treasury was unprecedented then and would be considered a miracle now."

*The dome of
the capitol
in Atlanta.*

The capitol rotunda serves as a Georgia Hall of Fame, with pictures of governors and other outstanding Georgians. The Georgia State Museum of Science and Industry on the capitol's fourth floor is "perhaps unequaled by any state."

Another outstanding institution is the Atlanta Museum. One of its most fascinating exhibits is the original cotton gin of Eli Whitney. Another is the first Japanese *Zero* airplane captured by the United States in World War II. The museum is housed in the last remaining large mansion on Peachtree Street.

The Atlanta Art Association has a reputation as one of the most advanced and outstanding organizations of its type. Its museum is also on Peachtree Street. Another prized cultural organization of the city is the Atlanta Symphony.

In spacious Grant Park is the remarkable Cyclorama. This is one of the largest oil paintings ever created. It has been mounted in a large circular room (400 feet [122 meters] in circumference) in its own building. The painting shows the action of the Battle of Atlanta at 4:30 P.M. on July 22, 1864, as General Benjamin Cheatham counterattacked, trying to restore his line. Actual figures and other three-dimensional parts of the diorama help to give the visitor the feeling that he is standing in the midst of the actual battle, with Old Abe, the Wisconsin regiment's eagle mascot, screaming overhead. In display at the Cyclorama Building is the famous locomotive *Texas*.

Another feature of Grant Park is its zoo. Atlanta is renowned for its parks, especially in spring when the dogwood everywhere flutters its waxy bloom. Chastain Memorial Park, Lakewood, Adams, and Piedmont are other Atlanta parks.

The Atlanta of today has constant programs for civic improvement. As early as 1926 Atlanta began its modern movement with a "Forward Atlanta" campaign. This was conducted with the largest expenditure for national advertising ever made by any city up until that time. The success of the campaign was shown by the fact that almost six hundred major firms established headquarters or branches in the city within the next three years.

Modern Atlanta is one of the nation's most dynamic and fast-developing cities.

The city's leading thoroughfare, Peachtree Street, likes to be considered the "Mainstreet of the South." In a drugstore on Peachtree Street the world's first Coca-Cola was served. Where Peachtree meets other streets in what is called Five Points is now the heart of Atlanta's business district. Today, luxury shops and skyscrapers elbow one another for room. Rich's Department Store is one of the nation's leading emporiums.

The old Governor's Mansion on Peachtree Street became unsafe in 1921 and was torn down. The present mansion of the governor is built of native stone atop a high hill overlooking pleasant subdivisions and with a view of both Kennesaw and Stone mountains. It occupies a site where breastworks were built in 1864 for the defense of Atlanta.

Another notable building of the city is the majestic Co-Cathedral of Christ the King. The Municipal Auditorium, built in 1908, seats 5,000 and was improved and air-conditioned in 1953. The million dollar, 14-story City Hall was built in 1929.

Atlanta monuments include the Henry Grady Monument, dedicated to the newspaper man who was one of the most helpful promoters of his native state, the Booker T. Washington Monument, and the fine Peace Monument, with the figure of the Goddess of Peace calling upon a Confederate soldier to lower his gun.

Today it stands as a reminder that the states of both the North and the South are reunited in the country's common goals.

Handy Reference Section

Instant Facts

Became the 4th state, January 2, 1788
Capital—Atlanta, settled 1813
Nickname—The Empire State of the South or Peach State
State motto—*Wisdom, Justice, and Moderation*
State bird—Brown thrasher
State fish—Largemouth bass
State flower—Cherokee rose *(Rosa sinica)*
State tree—Live oak
State song—"Georgia On My Mind," by Hoagy Carmichael
State waltz—"Our Georgia," words and music by James B. Burch
Area—58,876 square miles (152,488 square kilometers)
Rank in area—21st
Greatest length (north to south)—315 miles (507 kilometers)
Greatest width (east to west)—250 miles (402 kilometers)
Geographic center—Twiggs, 18 miles (29 kilometers) southeast of Macon
Highest point—4,784 feet (1,458 meters), Mt. Enotah, known as Brasstown Bald
           Mountain
Lowest point—Sea level
Population—1980 census: 5,464,265 (1985 estimate: 5,976,000)
Population density—95 persons per square mile (36 persons per square
           kilometer), 1980 census

Principal cities—	1980 Census	1984 Estimate
Atlanta	425,022	426,100
Columbus	169,441	174,800
Savannah	141,658	145,000
Macon	116,896	120,200
Albany	74,425	85,000
Augusta	47,532	46,000

You Have a Date with History

1540—Exploration of Hernando de Soto
1560—Tristan de Luna, with 300 soldiers, explores north Georgia for gold
1565—Pedro Menendez sent to drive out French
1566—First Spanish mission established on St. Catherines Island
1670—English and French declare Georgia to be neutral ground
1689—Spanish abandon all Georgia missions
1721—First English settlement of present-day Georgia
1733—Oglethorpe establishes colony of Georgia
1742—Battle of Bloody Marsh destroys Spanish claims to region
1754—King takes over Georgia as Royal Province
1775—Georgia delegates finally seated at Continental Congress

1777—Initial state constitution adopted
1778—Savannah captured by British
1782—Americans recapture Savannah
1785—University of Georgia chartered
1788—Statehood
1795—Louisville becomes capital
1819—*City of Savannah* sails for Liverpool
1827—Last of Creek Indian lands ceded to Georgia
1828—Gold discovered in northern Georgia
1838—Last of Cherokee leave Georgia over the Trail of Tears
1842—Dr. Crawford W. Long first to use ether as anesthetic
1861—Fort Pulaski seized, secession ordinance approved, Confederate
        Constitution adopted
1862—Federal forces retake Fort Pulaski
1863—Federal defeat at Battle of Chickamauga
1864—Sherman takes, burns, Atlanta; occupies Savannah
1865—Jefferson Davis captured near Irwinville; secession ordinance repealed
1867—Military occupation of Georgia
1868—New state constitution; Atlanta new capital
1872—"Reconstruction" ends in Georgia
1881—International Cotton Exposition
1886—Coca-Cola originated in Atlanta
1889—Capitol building dedicated
1912—Girl Scouts organized at Savannah
1918—93,321 men had served in World War I
1922—Georgia gives nation first woman senator
1927—Warm Springs Foundation established by F.D.R.
1937—*Gone With the Wind* takes Pulitzer Prize
1945—President Franklin D. Roosevelt dies at Warm Springs
1946—320,000 Georgians had served in World War II
1952—Atlanta annexes 82 square miles (212 square kilometers) of territory
1956—State flag adopted
1962—Nuclear ship *Savannah* visits namesake city
1966—Atlanta becomes home of baseball Braves
1972—Stone Mountain monument completed
1973—Maynard H. Jackson Jr. becomes first black mayor of Atlanta
1977—Jimmy Carter, from Plains, becomes U.S. president
1983—A new constitution becomes effective
1986—First national observance of the birthday of Martin Luther King, Jr.
        of Atlanta
1987—Democratic governor Joe Frank Harris begins second term following
        landslide re-election.

Sailboats on Lake Sidney Lanier in northern Georgia.

Governors of the State (since statehood)

George Handley 1788-1789
George Walton 1789
Edward Telfair 1789-1793
George Mathews 1793-1796
Jared Irwin 1796-1798
James Jackson 1798-1801
David Emanuel 1801
Josiah Tattnall, Jr. 1801-1802
John Milledge 1802-1806
Jared Irwin 1806-1809
David B. Mitchell 1809-1813
Peter Early 1813-1815
David B. Mitchell 1815-1817
William Rabun 1817-1819
Matthew Talbot 1819
John Clark 1819-1823
George M. Troup 1823-1827
John Forsyth 1827-1829
George R. Gilmer 1829-1831
Wilson Lumpkin 1831-1835
William Schley 1835-1837
George R. Gilmer 1837-1839
Charles James McDonald 1839-1843
George Walker Crawford 1843-1847
George Washington Towns 1847-1851
Howell Cobb 1851-1853
Herschel Vespasian Johnson 1853-1857
Joseph Emerson Brown 1857-1865
James Johnson 1865
Charles Jones Jenkins 1865-1868
Gen. Thomas H. Ruger 1868
Rufus Brown Bullock 1868-1871
Benjamin Conley 1871-1872
James Milton Smith 1872-1877

Alfred Holt Colquitt 1877-1882
Alexander H. Stephens 1882-1883
James Stoddard Boynton 1883
Henry D. McDaniel 1883-1886
John Brown Gordon 1886-1890
William J. Northen 1890-1894
William Y. Atkinson 1894-1898
Allen Daniel Candler 1898-1902
Joseph M. Terrell 1902-1907
Hoke Smith 1907-1909
Joseph Mackey Brown 1909-1911
Hoke Smith 1911
John Marshall Slaton 1911-1912
Joseph Mackey Brown 1912-1913
John Marshall Slaton 1913-1915
Nathaniel E. Harris 1915-1917
Hugh Manson Dorsey 1917-1921
Thomas W. Hardwick 1921-1923
Clifford Walker 1923-1927
Lamartine G. Hardman 1927-1931
Richard B. Russell, Jr. 1931-1933
Eugene Talmadge 1933-1937
Eurith Dickinson Rivers 1937-1941
Eugene Talmadge 1941-1943
Ellis G. Arnall 1943-1947
Melvin E. Thompson 1947-1948
Herman Eugene Talmadge 1948-1955
S. Marvin Griffin 1955-1959
Samuel E. Vandiver, Jr. 1959-1963
Carl E. Sanders 1963-1967
Lester G. Maddox 1967-1971
James E. Carter 1971-1975
George D. Busbee 1975-1983
Joe Frank Harris 1983

Index

PICTURE CREDITS

Color photographs courtesy of the following: Stone Mountain Memorial Association, pages 9 and 11; Department of Natural Resources, 15, 58, and 91; USDI, NPS Ocmulgee National Monument, 18; Georgia Bureau of Industry and Trade, Tourist Division, 20, 26, 29, 41, 46, 50, 60, 67, 73, 74, 81, and 87; Architect of the U.S. Capitol, 32; Department of the Army, Mobile District, Corps of Engineers, 34; University of Georgia Cooperative Extension Service, 52 (top); U.S. Department of Agriculture, Robert Hailstock, Jr., 52 (bottom); The University of Georgia, Office of Public Relations, 70, Historic Sites Survey, 78.

Illustrations on back cover by Len W. Meents.

ABOUT THE AUTHOR

With the publication of his first book for school use when he was twenty, **Allan Carpenter** began a career as an author that has spanned more than 135 books. After teaching in the public schools of Des Moines, Mr. Carpenter began his career as an educational publisher at the age of twenty-one when he founded the magazine *Teachers Digest.* In the field of educational periodicals, he was responsible for many innovations. During his many years in publishing, he has perfected a highly organized approach to handling large volumes of factual material: after extensive traveling and having collected all possible materials, he systematically reviews and organizes everything. From his apartment high in Chicago's John Hancock Building, Allan recalls, "My collection and assimilation of materials on the states and countries began before the publication of my first book." Allan is the founder of Carpenter Publishing House and of Infordata International, Inc., publishers of *Issues in Education* and *Index to U.S. Government Periodicals.* When he is not writing or traveling, his principal avocation is music. He has been the principal bassist of many symphonies, and he managed the country's leading non-professional symphony for twenty-five years.

96